SINGAPORE, MY COUNTRY

Biography of
M. Bala Subramanion

SINGAPORE, MY COUNTRY

Biography of M. Bala Subramanion

Nilanjana Sengupta

WS Professional

NEW JERSEY • LONDON • SINGAPORE • BEIJING • SHANGHAI • HONG KONG • TAIPEI • CHENNAI • TOKYO

Published by

WS Professional, an imprint of
World Scientific Publishing Co. Pte. Ltd.
5 Toh Tuck Link, Singapore 596224
USA office: 27 Warren Street, Suite 401-402, Hackensack, NJ 07601
UK office: 57 Shelton Street, Covent Garden, London WC2H 9HE

Library of Congress Control Number: 2016023453

National Library Board, Singapore Cataloguing-in-Publication Data
Name(s): Sengupta, Nilanjana.
Title: Singapore, my country : biography of M. Bala Subramanion / Nilanjana Sengupta.
Description: Singapore : WS Professional, [2016]
Identifier(s): OCN 944933415 | ISBN 978-981-31-4129-2 (paperback) |
    ISBN 978-981-31-4128-5 (hardcover)
Subject(s): LCSH: M. Bala Subramanion. | Postmasters general--Singapore--Biography. |
    East Indians--Singapore--Biography. | Singapore--History.
Classification: LCC HE7241.A6 | DDC 383.492--dc23

Copyright © 2016 by World Scientific Publishing Co. Pte. Ltd.

All rights reserved. This book, or parts thereof, may not be reproduced in any form or by any means, electronic or mechanical, including photocopying, recording or any information storage and retrieval system now known or to be invented, without written permission from the publisher.

For photocopying of material in this volume, please pay a copying fee through the Copyright Clearance Center, Inc., 222 Rosewood Drive, Danvers, MA 01923, USA. In this case permission to photocopy is not required from the publisher.

On the cover, from left:
A typical red pillar post box, introduced by the British in Singapore in 1873.
Masks & Dances, the first set of definitive stamps of Singapore, issued in December 1968.
The Fullerton Building which housed the General Post Office.

Stamp images on the cover are reproduced with permission from the Singapore Philatelic Museum.

Desk Editor: Shreya Gopi

Typeset by Stallion Press
Email: enquiries@stallionpress.com

To my daughter, Ananya,
To whom we bequeath the mixed legacy of migration

Acknowledgements

I remain grateful to Ambassador K Kesavapany, my mentor and friend, a diplomat with a litterateur's heart, for giving me this book. It compelled me to look at my city with new eyes and it was almost like wandering into a secret society — contemporary structures seemed marked by holograms all but invisible to others. Where others saw retail chains, I saw mullioned verandas and a glittering cupola; where others saw the city's conduit to commerce, I saw a boxing ring where Chua Lai had sparred with Kid Gabo; where others saw the first Asian Postmaster-General, I saw a man who owed his life and his lost pleasures to Singapore's culture of meritocracy.

I would like to thank Professor Edwin Thumboo for permission to use excerpts from his poems in this book.

Nilanjana Sengupta
Singapore, 2016

The publication of this book has been made possible by a generous grant from philanthropist, Mr S M Abdul Jaleel, BBM, PBM.

Proceeds from the sale of this book will be donated to the Singapore Indian Association's Welfare Fund.

Foreword

As one moves through the tapestry of Bala Subramanion's life-story, as narrated by Nilanjana Sengupta, one becomes conscious of the fact that the fabric that is woven here has three distinct strands held together by a common thread. First, of course, there is the story of Bala Subramanion, a man who from modest beginnings reached the very top of his chosen career. For the reader this story is the most interesting and it is also the common thread that holds all three stories together.

It is a heartwarming, personal story, firmly rooted in the history of an evolving Singapore. As one progresses through the book one cannot help but notice the similarities which mark the histories of man and nation. Like Singapore, Bala overcame tremendous odds to rise to the top. He faced adversities with great fortitude. The poignant moments in his life, like when he lost his son, Bala handled with calm and was a tower of strength for his bereaved family.

Encircling Bala and also forming the second strand of narrative in the book, is the story of the Singapore Postal Department and its offspring the Post Office Savings Bank. The book delineates the department's commendable journey from being just a service provider of mail and parcel delivery to becoming a significant partner in the economic and communications boom that has overtaken the country today.

And finally there is the story of the Indian community of Singapore from colonial days to the present. Bala's life reflects the many changes that have taken place in the community which in a way moved in tandem with the progress in Bala's life. Just to illustrate this point I would like to narrate an anecdote about an experience I had in 1962 when I was a young teacher in Raffles Institution. I was given the task of marking essays submitted for a competition on the theme of "Nation Building". One of the students had written about the contribution of the three main races. After discussing the Chinese and Malays, he had this to say of the Indians: "Of course we should not forget the Indians. Without them who would sweep our roads and clean our drains." This was how Indians were perceived in the 1960s. From there to the present times when Indians occupy responsible positions in the fields of politics, law, education, judiciary, IT, banking, etc., has been yet another commendable journey. A journey made possible due to the indefatigable efforts at community building of pioneers such as Bala Subramanion as well as the meritocratic system put in place in Singapore by its founding fathers.

One of the most appealing characteristics of the book is that its author, Nilanjana Sengupta, has done deep research to ensure that the biography is well contextualised within the history of Singapore. The Indian Association under the leadership of Ambassador Kesavapany is to be commended for taking the initiative to start this series of biographies of people like Bala who have contributed significantly to Singapore's growth and who are today role models for the younger generation. Most importantly, I want to congratulate Bala for allowing his life-story to be written as he saw its deeper significance and I congratulate Nilanjana for providing an interesting narrative of a multifaceted story.

Ambassador Gopinath Pillai
Ambassador-At-Large
Ministry of Foreign Affairs
Singapore

Message

When I think of the many people who have helped make Singapore what it is today, perhaps not adequately recognised for their contributions, the following verse from Gray's elegy comes to my mind:

> *"Full many a gem of purest ray serene*
> *The dark unfathom'd caves of ocean bear:*
> *Full many a flower is born to blush unseen,*
> *And waste its sweetness on the desert air."*

One such person is the subject matter of this book, Mr M Bala Subramanion. It was only after I became involved in the affairs of the Singapore Indian Association six years ago that I came to know of the full extent of his contributions to the nation and the community. He sought me out like many others to help him rebuild the Association which had unfortunately fallen on hard times. It was with his persistence, incidentally a hallmark of his character, that we were inspired to reposition SIA as a more responsive partner of the community. He is particularly interested in welfare, being a long-standing member of the Associations' Welfare Fund. Characteristically, he has decided to pledge the proceeds from the sale of this book to the Fund.

It is my honour and pleasure to have been the catalyst to this biographical enterprise which has been brought to fruition with Nilanjana's contributions and the active assistance of Mrs Sumitra B Subramanion. I hope this book will receive the welcome it deserves from all quarters of the society.

Mr K Kesavapany
President
Singapore Indian Association

Contents

Acknowledgements   vii
Foreword   ix
Message   xi
Endorsements   xv

Chapter 1   My Neighbour is Another Language   1

Chapter 2   Nothing without Labour   32

Chapter 3   How You Wrestled Nippon-go Far into the Night   57

Chapter 4   Gave Him a Cause   94

Chapter 5   Restore this Sun to us and the Waiting Generations   141

Chapter 6   We Must Make a People   195

Endorsements

Seen from the unique perspective of Mr Bala Subramanion's recollections of life in the early days of Singapore, Singapore, My Country presents a fascinating account of the many hurdles Mr Bala faced in his life while Singapore was still in the process of forging its national identity. The book captures how he overcame the odds after starting work as a postal clerk in 1936 to rise to become the first Asian Postmaster-General of Singapore and his vision that led to the transformation of the postal services.

Nilanjana Sengupta deserves credit for her patience and perseverance in the tedious work of gathering facts, looking at old records, sifting through photographs, locating and catching up with many long lost individuals acquainted with Mr Bala and painstakingly putting together this book which makes for compelling reading.

The book is a treasure trove of memories that will captivate the reader and bring to focus one man's amazing journey from a village boy to being the key driver of a government institution that shaped the communication infrastructure of Singapore.

Mr Ameerali Abdeali, JP
President
Muslim Kidney Action Association

The Fullerton Hotel, the Old General Post Office — Mr Bala Subramanion's presence and smile are reflected in that space. I am extremely fortunate to be a friend of this kind-hearted, grand Postmaster-General who served Singapore for more than an era.

It is still very fresh in my memory, the day that he requested my late husband Mr Bhaskar for photographs of a Bharatha Natyam dancer and a Kathakali dancer's face, to be used on a Singapore stamp. Mr Bhaskar took my photograph and passed it to Mr Bala together with one of our Kathakali master's photos. At that time, Singapore was celebrating the diversity of her culture through postal stamps. We felt proud and honoured to be a part of Singapore's postal history.

My heartfelt gratitude to Mr Bala. We will always cherish his friendship and his passion towards the Indian traditional arts.

Mrs Santha Bhaskar
Artistic Director
Bhaskar's Arts Academy

Nilanjana Sengupta has written a very inspiring story of a modest young Indian who grew up in pre-war Singapore and his remarkable journey in life that took him to the top spot in the Postal Services Department, culminating in his appointment as the first Singaporean Postmaster-General.

I had the privilege of working in the Postal Services Department under Mr Bala. He was my first boss, mentor and now my friend. During his tenure, Mr Bala was responsible for the management of the Post Office Savings Bank (POSB). Not many people are aware that he was the Chairman of the Savings Bank Advisory Committee that took the first steps to re-shape and transform the POSB to the iconic household brand that it is today, touching the lives of almost every Singaporean. Apart from his career achievements, Mr Bala also made his mark in uplifting the Indian community of Singapore. Despite his advanced age, he continues to be actively engaged in a range of social activities involving the Indian community.

Mr Bertie Cheng
Chairman
TeleChoice International Ltd.
Formerly CEO of the POSBank and currently Advisor to POSB

Singapore, My Country is the story of a life of an illustrious son of Singapore spanning over nine decades. There are so many interesting tales starting with Singapore as a British colony through the days of Japanese Occupation between 1942 and 1945, and the short period of Malaysia until independence in 1965. A book from which much can be learned of the history of Singapore in the last almost hundred years, from a single, devoted Singaporean.

Mr Koh Seow Chuan
Architect
and Stamp and Art Collector

Although Bala and I would have worked in the same Grand Old Lady that was the Fullerton Building, now the magnificent Fullerton Hotel, during the 1960s and part of the 1970s, I do not recall our paths ever crossing. What a pity. Now well into his tenth decade, Bala could have been a wise guide to a rookie like me in those early days of my Civil Service career. Later I got to know Bala a little more intimately, and was struck by his unfailing good humour, patience with all and sundry, and willingness to share his wisdom with others in a non-intrusive manner. He did not bore listeners with hoary tales of little consequence from the past. He was measured and prudent in whatever he turned his attention to. We look forward to celebrating with him and his family when he reaches his century, a crowning achievement in a life worthily led.

Mr J Y Pillay
Rector
College of Alice & Peter Tan
National University of Singapore

I am happy to see that the Singapore Indian Association has taken the initiative to commission the writing of the biography of Mr Bala Subramanion, a highly respected member of the Indian Community, my elder and dear friend. This book is certainly a very valuable addition to the repertoire of books available on Singapore. It narrates in lucid prose the story of one of the pioneers, who has played a critical role, not only as a civil servant in his various appointments but also in shaping a number of social and community-based intitutions in Singapore. For older people like me, the book brings back past memories, and hopefully for the younger generations, provides an opportunity to learn the fascinating reappraisal of history. I hope Mr Subramanion's story of ceaseless endeavour and enterprise will inspire many.

Mr Haider Sithawalla
Director
KSP Investments Pte Ltd.

M Bala Subramanion draws us to open our hearts as we admire his forte, his strength of character. Nilanjana's finesse captures his life and makes his biography a captivating read. For it was not the suffering that enabled his willpower, but the very joys which perseverance would bring. He embodies these qualities not only for himself but for the less fortunate individuals of the Indian community.

"All the world's a stage, and all the men and women merely players: they have their exits and their entrances in his life. And one man in his time plays many parts".

As we watch my grandfather undertake the many 'parts', it is for us, the younger generation, to understand and appreciate such benevolence and fortitude, and the motivation to achieve the impossible. For the world needs more intellectually vivacious individuals like my Thatha (grandfather).

Ms Hannah Divya Thomas
Granddaughter of M Bala Subramanion

The biography of Mr M Bala Subramanion provides valuable insights into the most important junctures of Singapore history. He rose to eminence from being a humble employee of the colonial postal service to becoming the Postmaster-General of Singapore at the time of Singapore's independence. It was at that level of recognition that he was held when I first heard of him from Tun V T Sambanthan, Malaysian Minister of Works, Posts and Telecommunications in 1968. As an undergraduate at the University of Malaya, I dismissed the fond mention of Mr Bala as one of those who never related themselves to the plight of non-English speaking working class Tamils in Singapore. However, by the time I joined the Tamils Representative Council in 1981, Mr Bala was contributing as Chairman of its Education Committee, working for the advancement of Tamil language in our schools. I was fortunate to have worked with him for seven years promoting the educational welfare of Indian youths across Singapore. He is one of those who rose to high positions in Singapore, but never forgot to give back to society by helping the underprivileged. The book not only details the life and times of one of the illustrious men who made Singapore, but also the way he navigated himself in caring for the nation and his community.

Professor Mani, A (A Veeramani)
Ritsumeikan Asia Pacific University, Japan &
Visiting Senior Fellow, ISEAS-Yusof Ishak Institute, Singapore

The Fullerton Building witnessed the incredible transformation of Singapore as the nation's modern history unfolded. From being the centre of Singapore as Mile Zero, to being the centre of communications as a General Post Office and the centre of commerce where important government offices were housed, the building stood as a testament to the Singapore Spirit from the colonial era to pre-war and modern age. In the very same *way, Mr Bala Subramanion's life story is one that speaks of tenacity and the will to not only survive but to thrive. We are heartened that Mr Bala's biography will add on to the treasure trove of precious memories and rich heritage. Indeed, it is a legacy that will impart the many narratives of the Singapore Story to our present and future generations.*

Mr Giovanni Viterale
General Manager
The Fullerton Heritage

Chapter 1

My Neighbour is Another Language

Early Days: 1917–1935

"Having left Mountain Head through
Lower Gate for these Southern Seas,
They miss morning's children-laughter
…The temperature is charged; the evening sky
Has more colours, but no crags to help it glow.
Moods re-arrange. Ink flows with a second spirit.
Stars have new names; winds rise into a rolling,
Plaintive call; strange incense fills the air.
You hear water swish when caged carps breath;
Ripples where crabs slip tactfully into pure stillness.
No crocuses in spring; no spring; no plum blossoms
Waiting for a poet. Only spider orchids for company
In a land where man-in-nature is a different history
My neighbour is another language."

Arts House, Smith Street, Chinatown, Singapore
— Edwin Thumboo

Between Sleep and Waking

It was the death of night, the time before dawn when the dark was really dark and the silence really silent.

His mother said a *kampong* (village) like theirs had no secrets. Yet it was the time of night when the *lorongs* around their house seemed shrouded in mystery, soft-footed shadows chased each other and the hush was broken only by the occasional hoot of an owl.[1]

Bala lay on his side with his palm tucked under his cheek, his pillow still damp from the tears he had shed. From where he lay, next to his sleeping mother and sister, he faced the only window of their room. He watched the clouds shift, now taking on the shape of a ghoul, now an ogre, dimly outlined against a sky which he called *vaanam* at home but *langit* when with his friends.[2]

In a few hours from now a man from the *Singapore Gas Works* would come to turn off the street lamps. He would scamper up the ladder, his white *veshti* hauled up and tightly knotted around his waist like a loin cloth, exposing brown muscular thighs.[3] He always appeared to be in a hurry in the early dawn, as if willing himself to melt into the shadows before the bustling day began — a faintly ludicrous figure against the solemnity of the rising sun.

Feeling restless, Bala leaned over and reached for the jars of Siamese fighting fish which he kept hidden under the bed. He could barely see their outline but could feel them intuitively flaring up their colourful fins as one encountered the other across the glass walls of the jars... Bala, for the first time in the night felt a smile curling the corners of his mouth.

In his mind he once again went over the events of the day before, the shrillness of the bell announcing the end of school. Bala had emerged from a history lesson feeling rather disoriented, his mind still full of England, half expecting the Battle of Waterloo to be unravelling around him. Instead he had found himself caught in a tropical shower, as dramatic as the battle itself with lightning tearing at the sky and palm fronds caught in a frenzy, like devotees in a spell of hysterical ecstasy at the Kaliamman Temple. He had quickly hailed a rickshaw and felt rather grand as he travelled atop it down Serangoon Road. He dismounted in front of his home and waited for his mother to give the rickshaw puller the 5 cents fare, least expecting the reception that awaited him inside.

His angry father had slapped him hard across his face, saying there was no need to waste money on a rickshaw when he was struggling to make ends meet and added, back in India children were not like this, they listened to their parents, respected the wishes of elders.

As, to his immense embarrassment, unmanly tears coursed down his cheeks, Bala felt a trifle perplexed. For just a week back when he had come home walking, drenched from another unexpected downpour, hadn't his mother told him much the same thing? She had slapped him hard and said, why couldn't he take a rickshaw when it was raining so hard? Wasn't it easier to pay the 5 cents as rickshaw fare rather than the few dollars they would now have to pay to the *kai vaithiyar* when he fell sick?[4] Children in India were not like this, they understood their parents' problems and scarcely if ever allowed money to be frittered away.

It made Bala wonder if his parents actually knew how children in India behaved. Or were the children of India born with some special magical prowess that children in these parts of the world did not possess? An invisible umbilical cord which connected them forever to their land and its laws which gave them an automatic, instinctual superiority?

Bala tried hard to conjure up pictures of India in his mind. Thanjavur in Southern India from where his father had come long years back, a city on the shores of the Kaveri River. Thanjavur — a name which was rich with the sound of temple bells. He rolled the name over and over on his tongue like a piece of candy. It filled him with a certain sense he could not really put his finger on. Was it a sense of wellbeing? The same sense of contentment he felt when he managed to catch a kite spiralling down from the sky? He tried to take his mind back to that early morning when his father as a youth had arrived at the Nagapattinam Port to take a ship to Malaya, his few possessions tied up in a piece of cloth under his arm.

But the pictures faded before emerging, like a roll of film which was on fast forward. Instead, all he could see was the greenish water of Singapore's Rochor Canal, serene under an early morning mist. Angsana trees lined its shore, an occasional woman from the neighbourhood stood bent over, sieving salt from the seawater that flowed in during high tide. His friends in white singlet and khaki shorts were running helter-skelter down the canal's bank. Their feet seemed to fly through the puddles, mud rising from the ground in a thick, dark brown sludge as they ran after kites, screaming, "*Potong! Potong! Potong!*"[5]

Kampong Potong Pasir and First Rules of Growing Up

Bala does not have too many intimate memories of his father. All he remembers is that he was an intensely private man with few friends. He liked keeping to himself and was often away on business. At home, Bala and his two sisters maintained a careful distance from him — two generations inhabiting two different worlds with a seemingly unbridgeable distance between them.

Bala's father, V Murugasu, had migrated from the town of Kumbakonam, in Thanjavur District of Southeast India, to the Federated Malay States (FMS) when in his late 20s. From the little they know about the migration story, it had been an impetuous decision of a young man who had had for some reason, be it poverty or otherwise, decided to bid adieu to his own country and instead embark on a long, lonely journey to a foreign land in search of greener pastures. His ship crossed the Indian Ocean, entered the Straits of Malacca and dropped anchor at Penang, where he was held for a week or so under the compulsory quarantine regulation. Thereafter, he started a business in petty trade, plying between Singapore and Malaya on work. During his growing up years Bala would either see him working as an itinerant salesman or at times he would travel with groups of European tourists to Batavia of the Dutch East Indies, the Anglo-Dutch Treaty of 1824 having allowed British subjects of the Malay Peninsula travel and trade access to Indonesia. Presumably during one of his trips to Malaya, he met and later married Rajambal from Kajang, a town in the eastern part of Selangor, and by 1915 settled down with her in Singapore.

Bala, i.e., M Bala Subramanion himself, was born on 5th March 1917 in a Singapore which was a British colony, a part of the Straits Settlements and like other port cities of the world, held a certain reputation for vice. As was customary, he was born at home with little celebration to mark the event, the first born of K Murugasu and Rajambal, daughter of Kailasam Pillai from Kajang.

A glance at the *Straits Times* of 5th March 1917 shows advertisements of 555 brand cigarettes selling at 75 cents for a tin of 50 and of the Danish Carlsberg Beer being available at John Little & Co, Raffles Place. Another commercial promises nickel- and silver-plated bedsteads "Specially built after 'PRANAKAN' taste" which have just been unpacked at the Julian Frankel Furniture Store of Orchard Road. Along with these, there is mention of wartime increase in food prices with British beef ribs having shot up by 66% and streaky bacon by 60% since 1st January 1914 — public notifications which are indicative of not only wartime difficulties but also of a deeply polarised society where the excesses of high living were not unknown to those who could afford it. It was a time when the racial supremacy of the British was meticulously maintained and even the whites were divided into various shades with corresponding social classes — the Eurasians of partially English origin, those of Portuguese origin and the ones of Ceylonese ethnicity or the Ceylon Burghers.

For the first year of his life Bala stayed in the village of Potong Pasir, off Upper Serangoon Road and down the hill from Woodsville. The Kallang River flowed in its undiminished glory through the village with Chinese vegetable farms dotting its shores and closed clusters of *kampong* houses nesting in the deep shade of banana, papaya and angsana trees.[6] The *attap* houses and fresh water ponds where Chinese and Malay farmers bred fish, were alive with the sound of quacking ducks and the loud calls of children. Around the estuary were the sand and granite quarries which gave Potong Pasir its name while nearby was the Bidadari Cemetery.[7] Situated on Mount Vernon Road, the cemetery served as a burial ground for all religious communities though Bala in his later life would particularly remember the Hindu processions — the pallbearers who would snake through the village carrying carbide lamps, chanting *mantras* in Tamil. The loud lamentation and beating of drums would strike fear in a child's heart.

The year 1917, the year of Bala's birth, is significant. It came too soon after the Sepoy Mutiny of 1915 when the 5th Light Infantry, the 800-strong Indian Muslim regiment garrisoned in Singapore, picked up arms against the British. Indian soldiers ran amok in the city with their cache of raided ammunition and finally 45 of them were sentenced to death. The execution of the rebels was done in full public view and the incident, though it did not garner support from the wider Indian community, turned on its head the long-held British understanding of Indian docility. Suddenly the role Indians had played as industrious intermediaries of the British was in question and new regulations were put in place to check for seditious activity among Indians. What this meant for a young man like Murugasu, struggling to feed a family in a foreign land which suddenly showed signs of becoming even more repressive towards his own kind, was to reach for that one tool which was freely available — caution. He became even more careful in his business dealings and imposed restrictions on his family to maintain a low-profile dexterity in conducting their lives' business. As Bala grew up there would be an increasing number of incidents when he was taken to task for what appeared to him a minor anomaly in his daily schedule. There was little tolerance for anything that resembled entertainment and he was encouraged to follow a daily routine of school study and chaperoned outings — occupations which were unobtrusive enough not to incur any unwarranted attention.

It will serve well to remember, Bala's early childhood was also a time when the free-trading status of colonial Singapore was rapidly changing. The colonial state was increasingly bringing under its net a port town which had been known to be the clearing house of travellers from around the world, where *chandu* was freely available, migrant workers from China poured in without too many stringent measures to check communist infiltration and brothels and cabarets enjoyed abundant clientele.[8] By the 1920s the colonial state was recognisably more direct and bureaucratic in its rule — secret societies had been banned, prostitution declared illegal, opium dens were fast disappearing and immigration and labour contracts were more closely supervised. In short, the foundation of the present day, more modern, disciplined state had been laid.

If Bala had a somewhat restrictive, closely supervised upbringing, it was in part a reflection of this changing culture of checks and balances which was emerging at the time. It was equally a throwback on Singapore's reputation as a tropical paradise of sensual squalor where a migrant family like Murugasu's would typically feel entrusted to uphold the moral code of their home country — the temple visits and dietary restrictions which became the most overt markers of Indian culture and which his parents felt compelled to champion in an overseas society. Along with this was the economic status of his father. As an itinerant salesman he fitted into that narrow band which enjoyed a precarious prestige in the migrant Indian community. Below him was the vast population of Indian labour who worked on the various public projects of Singapore — as dockers and cleaners, as coolies at the harbour, as night guards, as *dhobys* and cattlemen.[9] And above him was the service class — the doctors and lawyers, the engineers at the British-owned public utilities, and beyond that came the truly rich — the entrepreneurs and successful businessmen who could afford a life of high fashion at Orchard or Meyer Road. Murugasu, lacking in qualification to be an accredited "Company" employee and armed with only his command over the Queen's language, fitted into an amorphous, in-between category which the British census called "others". He eked out a difficult living and consequently guarded with a rare jealousy the toehold he had managed to achieve on the social ladder.

As Bala grew up it increasingly dawned on him that his father was not willing to allow his son's impetuosities to jeopardise this existence.

Sojourn to Seremban and Malacca

When Bala was around six years old Murugasu decided to shift base again, this time to Seremban in Malaya. The reason for this decision to move to the capital city of the state of Negeri Sembilan, well known for its rubber plantations and the Sungei Linggi or River Linggi which ferried tin from various trading posts to the Straits of Malacca, is not known. It is possible that Murugasu decided to move closer to his wife Rajambal's family in Kajang where her father ran an Indian restaurant because the young couple found it difficult to manage with their small son in the relatively more expensive Singapore. Or it could be that Murugasu, born with wanderlust, found it difficult to sink roots in one place and since he was in the habit of travelling to Malaya, Rajambal decided to follow suit. Whatever be the reason, the family stayed on in Seremban and subsequently in Malacca for the next six years, returning permanently to Singapore only in 1929. It was here that Bala's two younger sisters, considerably younger than him, were born. Yet even these six years were not an uninterrupted period of stay. Like many Tamils, the family maintained a fluidity of movement between Malaya and Singapore, a movement pattern that would continue till Singapore became independent in 1965. Only during the post-war period would a *jalan* pass or walking pass be issued to separate communist insurgents from residents. Before that, with the Johore Causeway inaugurated in 1923, British subjects were free to move between West Malaysia and Singapore.

But despite the family's prolonged sojourn to Malaya, they had little success in building a bond with Rajambal's family. Bala has no fond memories of indulgent grandparents or the maternal uncle who worked as a supervisor at a rubber plantation in Kajang. Theirs remained a nuclear family and later with the peripatetic nature of his job, Murugasu would be away for progressively longer periods, leaving Rajambal and her children largely to their own resources.

While in Seremban, Bala attended St Paul's Institution, the oldest English school of Negeri Sembilan. The school run by the Roman Catholic Lasallian Brothers or the *Brothers of the Christian Schools* was one of the many missionary schools being run by the brotherhood in Asia (in Singapore and Malaysia alone the count goes up to 34, including the Lasalle College of the Arts) and the future list of notable Paulians would include the Malay scholar Zailan Abidin Ahmad and S Rajaratnam, Minister for Foreign Affairs, Singapore.

In school Bala would close his morning prayers with an appeal to Saint Jean-Baptiste de La Salle with little understanding of the French teaching order or the canonized priest, Jean-Baptiste, or the fact that children in far off Madagascar or Mozambique would be praying much the same prayer and perhaps with the same amount of irreverence! During his time the school had as its Director, the Irish Bro. Lewis Edward who founded the St Paul's Athletic Association. Consequently the school had considerable focus on sports and during the day the school's make-shift assembly hall would double up as a sports field where boys played football and badminton.

But soon it was time to move again, this time to Malacca, the small Malayan state on the shores of the Straits of Malacca with a considerable Portuguese population. Perhaps this move was to facilitate Murugasu's tours to neighbouring Indonesia. In Malacca Bala went to the Anglo Chinese School, run this time by Methodist missionaries and he remembers the long distance he had to walk every morning to reach school. He felt rather ridiculous wearing the white cork *topee* which did not really fit his head and wobbled around embarrassingly. But the headgear, though it invited many a knocking knuckle from senior boys, was a school regulation as protection against sunstroke and so unavoidable.

What is remarkable about Bala's family stay in Malaya was that this was a period when two significant socio-political movements were gathering steam in the state. One was the incipient Tamil reform movement or the Self-Respect Movement which had strong Dravidian overtones and was gaining in popularity amongst the depressed classes, particularly estate labourers. This movement spoke about revival of the Tamil vernacular and uplifting the Adi Dravidas or the untouchables, and would peak with the visit of Ramasamy Naicker to Malaya in 1929. As opposed to this more sectarian, vernacular-based, anti-Brahmin movement was the Indian nationalist movement, inspired and guided by the Indian National Congress. By the very nature of its origin, this was more elitist, manned by English educated, urbane members of the society. Though in Malaya at this time the mass following of the Self-Respect Movement proved to be much larger than Gandhiji's brand of nationalism, Murugasu by opting for English medium schools for his children, consciously or otherwise, was siding more with the latter than the former. This was despite Rajambal's family connections with estate workers and possibly was aspirational on Murugasu's part. From personal experience he knew English to be the key to social success in a British colony. Interestingly, Tamil would continue to be perceived as lacking in commercial value (Turnbull commenting on this said, "Tamil schooling in Singapore offered no outlets for pupils except to become unskilled labourers") and later when Bala and his peers would realise the value of the Tamil reform movement in reinforcing cultural and linguistic connections to India, they would struggle to have the language associated with possibilities of career advancement.[10]

An anecdote that Bala is fond of narrating is from this period of his childhood. It was while the family was living in Malacca that a ten or eleven year old Bala got into the habit of following his friends to a local tennis club. They would make the most of sleepy weekend afternoons when their household was in a deliciously languorous state of stupor to make their way to the nearby club (in all probability Malacca Club). The self-appointed team leader would be waiting, having found a clever way to allow his friends into a club meant for the whites and the afternoon would be spent picking up discarded tennis balls which lay around the court. It was not an easy task, requiring some amount of manoeuvring around brambly bushes but the prize money of 5 or 10 cents as ball-picking fees would more than compensate for the difficulties. The money would jingle in his pocket, promising him a week of a daily stick of ice cream — all the more enjoyable because devoured in secrecy.

Interestingly, the incident did not provoke any untowardly response from Bala. It did not draw him into any unhappy comparisons between the lifestyle of the whites and the natives, the difference between the manicured expanse of the lawns and his own over-crowded home. He only felt a sharp stab of guilty pleasure as he fingered the coins in his pocket, a feeling that he remembers even today. Was it the natural obliviousness of a child? Or was this the proverbial docility of the colonised Indian, so prized by the British? Or was it the response of a child born in a migrant family, matured beyond his age who knew life to be unfair, that he would need some amount of stoical industriousness to get around it?

Return to Singapore

Though apparently Bala did not express any resentment at the tennis club incident, the sense of the simultaneous existence of two worlds, his own and that of the British elite which despite his own anglicised education he could not be a part of, remained with him. In fact, perhaps it was further sharpened as he returned to Singapore as a pre-adolescent. As he grew older there was a continual sense of the multiple worlds he needed to inhabit — the world behind the closed doors of his home where Rajambal wore the *pottu* on her forehead and insisted on following Tamil traditions, the world of his friends where he spoke a *bazaar* Malay and the outer world of the British where his formal English education came in handy.[11] As he grew older, assimilating the three worlds became a reflex response — the first was innermost, meant for the most private experiences, scarcely if ever aired in public, the second was important for social acceptance and expressing local solidarity, he would develop closer bonds with his Malay and Chinese friends as Asian bitterness towards the British grew, and the third he would associate with progress. Everything that was English would always be symbolical of evolution and advancement to him, a trait he shared with many subjects of the British empire. English was what gave him hope, a certain intrepidity, and later, even when he would look back at Tamil and seek social and religious reform, he would do so with his English trained sensibilities, borrowing the language of commerce for a very different purpose.

For Bala and his family, Singapore proved to be quite different from Malacca or Seremban right from the beginning. For one, the standards of living were better since the city had been a part of the Straits Settlements, administered directly by the colonial office in London from the start, and as such had seen considerable progress. Since 1923 the demand for tin, rubber and petroleum had been on the rise, the opening of the Johore Causeway had given new boost to trade and the price of tin had peaked by 1926-27. This translated into considerable increase in government spending and the improvement in public facilities was evident to all — the freshly enhanced Municipal Corporation, the new hospitals and maternity homes, the motorised public transport made available by the Singapore Traction Company and the first public housing provided by the government-financed Singapore Improvement Trust. Rooms at the Raffles Hotel, with its sea-facing ball room, dance-teas and whirring electric fans were available to the well-heeled tourist at $12 per night and *Hamlet* was staged at the Star Opera House, performed by a Malay troupe with an Ophelia boasting a dark mass of curls.[12]

But what was equally evident was the poor living conditions of the majority Indians, thrown into sharp focus by the affluent central districts meant for the white or the rich — Orchard Road lined by swaying traveller's palms and shop windows which glittered like a chimera, Tanglin and Bukit Timah with rows of white mansions and twinkling lattice windows. In contrast were the Indians — the *lascars*, the bricklayers, the *jamban* cleaners, emigrants mostly from the eastern shores of South India who were more visible in Singapore than in Malaya where they were safely ensconced in up-country plantations, tucked away from public view.[13] In Singapore, as they laboured at various public works projects and appeared policing important street junctions, they made for at best a timorous, perimetric presence. The Malays were the sons-of-the-soil, the Chinese had their loyalty to the Republic of China and the towering Sun Yat-sen, a unifying figure of post-imperial China. But the Indians seemed strangely rootless, yet another of Singapore's transient communities which, given the impoverished conditions it had left behind at home, seemed strangely unsure of where to transit to.

As he grew older, Bala was sensitised to the word *kling*, the indifferent moniker by which all South Indians were addressed (while North Indians came under the blanket term, *Bengalese*). That the term continued to wrankle is evident from references in local newspapers. Thus on 1 May 1917 (the year of Bala's birth), there appears an indignant letter from M Hariharam of Batu Anam who valiantly writes of the greatness of the Dravidian civilization which dates back from the "morning of the world" and is careful in distancing himself from the "dirty habits and stupidity of the Tamil coolie, who represents South India in this country." Yet again on 16 December 1927 appears a notification in the *Singapore Free Press & Mercantile Advertiser* (1884-1942). It begins with an explanation of the term, "the derelict or convict classes which could be well-spared from the mother-country and well-employed in the initial development of new land", and continues with the news of a certain Rev. J. Milton David, a British-Indian Tamil and a teacher at a Methodist school, who had managed to have the opprobrious term abolished from the records in Netherland East Indies. It was only later that Bala would come to know that *kling* was actually a mutated form of Kalinga, the ancient Indian kingdom whose most illustrious son was King Ashoka. But in his adolescence, to his untutored ears the name echoed only with the sound of the iron chains the Indian convicts were supposed to have worn when they were brought to the penal colony of Singapore, an onomatopoeic reflection on his community's not very memorable beginning. The writing on the wall, like moving shadow puppets, was gaining in clarity, emerging out of the miasma of marvel that is childhood and one wonders how it affected his emerging sense of self.

Murugasu decided to take up residence around the Serangoon Road area, that focal point of the Indian community to which every newcomer to the city veered in search of a familiar face or a home-cooked meal or a means to send back news to his family. As the 1920s waned, Singapore was sucked into the tidal wave of the Great Depression. It was a time when Singapore, like a camel, was living off its hump of an established shipping trade, when the future Prime Minister of Singapore, the late Lee Kuan Yew's father was compelled to take on a store keeper's job with Shell Oil Co. and the Indian businessman and philanthropist, R Jumabhoy, mortgaged seven of his houses for a meagre $ 60,000. For Bala, who would continue to live in this area for the next 20 years till 1949 when he left for the UK on a scholarship, this stay in the Serangoon Road area was like immersion training in his own culture. He came to be aware of a community which had arrived on the coattails of Sir Stamford Raffles when in 1825 the first Indian convict labourers arrived in Singapore from Bencoolen. It was quite the proverbial Noah's Ark, a medley of Benaras Brahmanas, Dogra Kshatriyas, Chettiars, Bengalis, Parsi financiers and the Adi Dravidas from all parts of the subcontinent. Some had stayed back and been assimilated into local culture, some had returned at the end of their prison term. But over the years the mainstay of the community had become the Tamils from Madras Residency, more so after the British government of the Straits Settlements & the FMS announced the Tamil Immigration Fund in 1908 which provided monetary aid in terms of train fares and steamship tickets to labourers and their families.

Around 1929 Murugasu and his family moved into a house in Rappa Terrace. In the middle of Rappa Terrace were a few elongated, single-storied houses. The house the family inhabited was actually a single room with corrugated partitions to delineate the kitchen, bedroom and bathroom, and had a single door which opened onto a veranda outside. The only difference with other dwellings in the vicinity was that it did not have a common cooking or washing facility or a *jamban* cleared by a night soil worker at the back.

Rappa Terrace was in between the two arterial lanes, Belilios Road and Klang Road which lead off Serangoon Road, overlooked by the Sri Veeramakaliamman Temple. A tour of the area undertaken in 1890 would have read like the following:

> "*The first junction on our left [on entering Serangoon Road from Rochor Canal Road, after crossing the Kandang Kerbau police station and post office] would be Buffalo Road. From here, past the junction of Kerbau Road and to the junction at Belilios Road, Serangoon Road was fronted by shophouses. A long stretch following from the Belilios Road junction to the Kinta Road junction [beyond Klang Road which hugs Rappa Terrace] was not built up — most probably due to the fact that the area was particularly low-lying and flood prone. Shophouses, this time interspersed with bungalows, reappear thereafter and continue past the junctions of Kinta Road, Roberts Lane, Birch Road, Burmah Road.... There were many ponds dotting this stretch.*"[14]

It was in this *particularly low-lying and flood prone* area which had seen some development in the years following 1890 that Murugasu rented a house with his family. The area took its name from one George Rappa Junior, a Eurasian middle-class entrepreneur, who had become the business partner of Philip Robinson (the founder of the Robinson's Department Store at Raffles Place) in 1859, and who in 1886 built a bungalow at the corner of Serangoon Road and Syed Alwi Road. Rappa Terrace lasted through the 1990s and it was only in 2002 that the Rappa Terrace shophouses were pulled down to build the Klang Lane HDB (Housing Development Board) block.

The area around Rappa Terrace was the domain of I R Belilios, a Venetian Jew who in all probability was from Calcutta, and was one of the foremost cattle kings of the area. In fact, the area around Serangoon Road and what forms today's Little India was dominated from the early decades by the cattle industry of Singapore. The vicinity was deemed particularly suitable because of the many fresh-water ponds which dotted the area around Race Course Road and the mangrove swamps of Kampong Kapor which came in handy for bathing the water buffaloes. Bala during his growing up years would have seen not only a proliferation of sheep pens and cow sheds in his neighbourhood but also the slaughter houses of Jalan Besar and Syed Alwi Road. In addition were other commercial concerns promoted by the cattle industry — the wheat-grinding sheds, sesame oil presses and rattan works, as well as the tannery industry around Serangoon Road. The sights and sounds of his neighbourhood would stay with him and shape his thinking — the tolling of the temple bell, the whine of the mill press, the North Indian *susuwalas* (milkmen) who made their way on a cycle and the lean-to shops in the alleyways which catered to all domestic emergencies.

Murugasu and Rajambal continued their strict vigil on their children's whereabouts as they felt there was much happening in the vicinity which could lead them astray. At the end of Kitchener Road was the open gateway to the New World cabaret where professional Chinese dancers could be hired for a few cents a dance and naval ratings gathered for a drink. In fact, closer home, at Kinta Road or Roberts Lane there were many barrack-style houses of young Indian bachelors (enforced or otherwise) who were the junior staff at cattle firms. They paid a few dollars a month for a bedroll atop the cattle quarters and were known to try their hand at gambling stalls.

Thus, carefully cordoned off from an environment about which his parents perhaps felt justifiably sceptical, Bala was left with very limited avenues of entertainment. There are a few scattered memories of visits to the Somapah Zoo run by the émigré W L S Basapa, the 'animal man', a man few messed with because of *Apay*, a full-grown Bengal tiger who was his constant companion, or to the fabled Alkaff Gardens which opened in 1929, located off MacPherson Road and named after the famous Yemeni Arab, Syed Shaikh bin Abdulrahman Alkaff.[15] It was built as a replica of a Japanese tea garden, complete with an artificial lake and a scaled-down Mt. Fuji. On such outings Murugasu would prefer to take his son but not his daughters and though they were not really family events with little warmth or bonhomie, Bala remembers them perhaps because they were rare occasions when he felt he was the chosen one, a little more special than others. He also remembers going for a few film shows with his father. Murugasu, by dint of his business dealings, would at times manage to get free high-class tickets which could have easily otherwise cost $2 or $2.50. Interestingly, Bala remembers watching two silent films at Surina Theatre, the upper-end cinema hall in North Bridge Road meant for the British — *Tarzan* and a wild western adventure — both fantasy adventures where the protagonist, a male, escapes oppressive circumstances by dint of considerable effort. One is tempted to wonder if this is a throwback on his own impotence in the face of adversity of which Bala was gradually becoming aware as he grew older. This theory could perhaps be taken a step further and connected to his fondness for playing with the colourful fighting fish he collected from the muddy ditches of the Race Course. He would keep them apart in separate glass jars and watch with glee as they tore at each other when brought together. Did games such as these satisfy a frustrated longing for action, an expression of a suppressed need to break free and prove himself? Maurice Baker, one of Singapore's pioneer diplomats, also mentions this hobby in his memoirs but it is Lee Kuan Yew who writes that the Siamese fish nurtured a fighting spirit in him, an important skill in his future political career.

By extension such incidents can be linked to yet another one which happened around the same time. Around this time, Singapore's newspapers carried regular articles about boxing matches which took place at the Lion City Ring. It was an open air stadium next to the Singapore Traction Company in Mackenzie Road, opposite Bukit Timah, where popular champions like Al Rivers, Sid Nash, Joe Diamond and Little Lewis displayed their skills. Alongside the stadium was a covered shed where the boxers practised and such practice sessions were popular with the youth since they could watch their icons spar for free. Bala was a regular spectator and enjoyed the discussions which followed when he and his friends conjectured about possible winners. But he yearned to watch an actual combat on the ring, knowing fully well that it was not a feasible dream. His parents would not agree to him remaining outside home in the late hours. Besides, they did not support any kind of sport and would never agree to finance such foolhardiness.

And then a surprise opportunity presented itself — some friends told him they had watched a match free of charge by climbing up a tree opportunely located opposite the stadium, along Bukit Timah Road and on the banks of the Rochor Canal. They apparently had a good view of the bouts and enjoyed the actual combating scenes and the echoes of spectator clamour. Bala had an open invitation to join them.

He thought of what seemed to him a plausible story — a friend's father was an usher at the stadium and would allow him in for public shows free of charge. Murugasu reluctantly agreed and what followed were a couple of evenings of undiluted and unaccustomed fun. But too soon the cat was out of the bag — a family friend unwittingly saw him clamber up the tree and promptly reported the episode to his parents. Murugasu did not spare the cane and Bala's passion for sparing bouts ended before it had really begun.

But those evenings remained with him, the golden sunset across Rochor Canal, the air pulsating with rolling applause, the triumphant champion holding up the trophy like a conquering emperor. Those were evenings when he had gritted his teeth and felt blood coursing through his veins, greedily ingesting the boxers' sense of determined purpose — a sense he would get to experience only much later in his long life.

Compulsions of a Good Boy

On returning to Singapore, Bala was admitted first to a Tamil medium school down Hastings Road. One wonders what the reason for such a decision was. Was it Rajambal's choice since she was very clearly the more traditional of the two parents, perceived by the children as the fountainhead of all things Tamil in the house? Or was it the proximity to so many Indian families in Serangoon Road which acted as a collective moral compulsion? Tamil medium schools had been available in Singapore since the second half of the 19th century, in fact, for a long time they were the only means of garnering an Indian vernacular education and had been gaining in prominence since the Dravidian Movement started. However, for Bala's family, vernacular intentions did not last long and by 1930, which means exactly after a year, he was admitted to the Royal English School. The major deterrent could have been the quality of education provided by such schools. As Turnbull rather scathingly points out, Tamil schooling provided few career opportunities to its pupils.

After admission to the Royal English School, Bala's predominantly westernised education continued and Tamil was relegated to the background, apart from the more superficial, ritualistic routines which were enforced at home by Rajambal. Consequently, he would remain largely unfamiliar with the ancient Tamil culture which had been in prevalence in the subcontinent since the time of the Proto-Dravidian spoken all over India before North India was swept clean of Dravidian antiquities by the Aryans. He would be little aware of his mother tongue which had travelled with sea-faring traders to the far off shores of Rome and Greece and left its mark in old Hebrew and Greek terms of commerce — classical Hebrew words like *tuki* or *ahalat* which bring to mind the Tamil *tokai* (total) or *akil* (wood). Bala would renew his ties with Tamil scholarship only in the 1960s when the freshly independent Singapore was intent on multilingualism. But for his two children, Anidha and Arjun, he would insist on basic Tamil skills before they learnt any other language. Anidha reminiscences of many a tedious Tamil lesson in school when the readers procured from India told of Indian stories and made little sense to her Singaporean ears, or of sitting through many a Tamil movie with her father who otherwise expressed little interest in Indian cinema. Any frivolity about the stars would not be entertained, instead, the focus remained firmly on getting up to speed in Tamil culture!

From 1930 to 1933 Bala studied at the Royal English School, a school with a bit of a controversial past. It was run by Francis

Neelankavil, the President of the Singapore Malayalee Association in 1926 — a man Bala remembers as a strict task master with a big paunch, who did not spare the stick. At the time of Bala's admission the school was located in Dhoby Ghaut, at the former site of the Cathay Building where there was a large Victorian-style house in which resided the family of the prominent businessman, Teo Hoo Lye. The building would be demolished in 1934 and the land cleared for constructing the Cathay Building. That there was some trouble brewing in the Royal English School is evident from a piece of news which surfaces in 1931: in December 1931 the local papers reported a row between Francis Neelankavil and one Miss N Samuel, a teacher at the Royal English School, over the issue of the payment of arrear salary which according to the teacher had been denied to her.

The school moved out of the Cathay site in 1931, after Neelankavil was served a legal notice to vacate the premises. Bala would travel with the school, first to Oldham Road, off Orchard and then to a renovated railway storage warehouse in Tank Road, off River Valley. But not surprisingly, given the indications of the newspaper report, the school would continue to be plagued by a dearth of senior teachers and Murugasu would finally decide to have Bala admitted to the newly opened Singapore English School in Oldham Road. Bala has few fond memories of the Royal English School except a class teacher, Mr Bhaskaran, who encouraged him to take part in school athletics. Bala emerged as quite a keen sportsman, bagging the medal for an 880-yard event at the annual sports day held in the stadium at Anson Road.

Bala joined the Singapore English School in 1933, passing his Junior Cambridge the same year, his Senior Cambridge in 1934 and the London Chamber of Commerce Examination in 1935. There appeared a notification in the *Straits Times* on 22 December 1936 of a Bala Subramanion passing the Chamber of Commerce Exam with book keeping, handwriting, typewriting and English, in which he was the only one from the school to have secured a distinction. His love for literature, which had lain mostly dormant for the last so many years, had blossomed in the Singapore English School under the tutelage of a North Indian English master who had previously taught at the Victoria Institution, Kuala Lumpur, Sapuran Singh Gill. He introduced Bala to the joys of reading Shakespeare, to the cadence of Keats and Byron and the evocative imagery of Scott. It was a passion that would stay with Bala, a strange bed fellow with his job in the P & T (Post and Telegraph) Department.

The Singapore English School also fed his other passion — sports. Managed by Frank Cooper Sands –Scoutmaster from Nottingham and founder of Scouting in Singapore and the Straits Settlements, who would later have the Scouts Headquarters in Armenian Street named after him — the school was careful in maintaining a high focus on athletics. Sapuran Singh also happened to be the physical education teacher and under him Bala participated in hockey, cricket and football matches. In 1935 he was selected the school athletic champion and the same year travelled to Kuala Lumpur as a member of the school football team. They played against the Victoria Institution, an eventful match which they unfortunately lost, and with the St John's Institution and a polytechnic school in KL. On 19 August 1935, there appears a reference to the last match in *Singapore Free Press & Mercantile Advertiser* (1884-1942), presumably alluding to the polytechnic school as a local trade school and mentioning the match which took place in the *Padang*.

Bala remembers going to and from school alone, the solitary occasion when his parents would allow him to be unaccompanied by an adult. He walked to school while his two sisters, Chandra Bai and Sulochana, who went to a school run by CEZMS or the Church of England Zenana Missionary Society on Mount Sophia (named after Raffles' second wife, Lady Sophia), were allowed to travel on a rickshaw. He would walk down Serangoon Road, crossing the beautiful Tekka Market, styled after the Covent Garden Market of London, cross the Rochor Canal area, bustling with food stalls and a line-up of rickshaws and bullock carts and hackney carriages and then turn, leaving the beautiful Ellison building and Colonial Bar to his left and walk towards Dhoby Ghaut which till not very long ago was home to the *dhobys* of Singapore, festooned with colourful washing fluttering on bamboo poles at all times of the day. If on the way he caught a glimpse of the posh Orchard Road or Tanglin, it would not bother him at all as he knew these places to be the haunt of the rich, aeons away from his own life. Trolley buses with hooter-happy Malay drivers would trundle past, fed by the overhead pantograph, again out of bounds for him because of high fares.[16] At school his studies were completely geared to serve the British Empire — he learnt arithmetic based on the English system of pounds, shillings and pence, and history lessons revolved around the famous Elizabethans, Sir Walter Raleigh or Oliver Cromwell. As he read poems like James Thomson's "Rule Britannia! Rule the waves: Britons never will be slaves", Bala was left in no doubt of the abiding power of the colonial masters.

Bala was allowed to escort his sisters to the Race Course grounds (today's Farrer Park) to play. The Race Course had been constructed in the early 1840s and the biannual horse-racing meet organised here provided a major diversion to the European community. The wooden stand was on the side of Serangoon Road and pedestrians outside could catch a glimpse of the horses and the well-heeled spectators. Earlier, Bala had learnt to play football when his parents had been on a trip to India, leaving him with a family that inhabited the domestic quarters on the grounds of the Government House or what is now the Istana. He would play bare foot on the muddy field with other boys living in the employee quarters of this 106-acre estate which had once formed a part of an extensive nutmeg plantation. Later, when his parents returned and took up residence around the Serangoon Road area, he continued to play football surreptitiously on the outer ring of the Race Course. He would take his sisters to play and leaving them to their girlie preoccupations, use the opportunity to indulge in a game with neighbourhood boys. He soon realised playing bare foot was not easy and some of the boys were already proud possessors of football boots. As with the boxing match, he was in a quandary — on one hand he desperately wanted to continue his secret love for the game and on the other hand knew his parents in all their parental inflexibility, would never agree to finance a pair of boots. Again, a good friend Samoo G came to his rescue, offering to not only buy him a pair of second-hand boots but also to keep them in his safe-keeping without the knowledge of Bala's parents. But where would the money, albeit reduced, come from? Bala again conceived a clever plan — he would save the amount from his daily pocket money of 10 cents! A torturous period followed, with him holding himself back from the daily fare of delicacies served by his school canteen so that at the end of the week he could hand over a fistful of coins to his saviour. At long last the wait was over and he could become the secret owner of a pair of football boots. But such were the pitfalls of wanting to remain on his parents' good books that even then he could not bring himself to share his triumph with them. And so remained secret an incident which spoke of a boy's quiet entrepreneurial spirit and cheery determination — qualities which would remain with him in the future.

The Mother of the Cremation Ground

Rajambal, like Murugasu, had migrated from Kumbakonam in Thanjavur, only one generation earlier. This meant her assimilation was deeper — she could speak fluent Malay and though she had Chinese friends, she found it difficult to pronounce their names and so gave them a Tamil name which was mutually acceptable, and so continued with her friendship. Being second generation also meant she was more adept at the reflex responses of a migrant — she was less overwhelmed than Murugasu by the strangeness of her surroundings, more self-assured in perpetuating certain rituals and traditions which she must have seen her mother observe. She accepted their sanctity because the sieving had already happened and rules laid down a generation before, unlike Murugasu who was still caught between memory and actuality and the shadow that each cast on the other. It was perhaps because of this that Rajambal appeared more strong and confident to her children than their father — she demanded unquestioning acquiescence.

Rajambal was the one who drew the festive *kolam* outside their main door to keep away evil spirits and fried *murukku* on Deepavali which the children then carried to their neighbours' houses.[17] Surprisingly, Bala barely remembers anything of such traditional practices which kept his *amma* (mother) thus preoccupied. He knew, at home he had to eat the *dosai* and *sambar* his mother made. If he happened to eat some Chinese porridge with a bit of dried fish on top from one of the women in a *samfu* who visited their locality carrying baskets of food slung on a pole, he knew he had to keep it a secret from his mother.[18] There was an altar at home where Rajambal placed fresh flowers every morning but Bala did not know which deity resided there. She made it a point to take him to the neighbourhood Veeramakaliamman Temple every Friday but he does not remember the reason. Deepavali remained for him a festival when they got to eat meat — perhaps the only day of the year when they could indulge in such luxury. It was also a time when he was gifted a pair of canvas shoes and some new singlets and shorts — his sartorial ration for the year. And Thaipusam was a time when he rushed to the street to see the colourfully decorated *kavadis* making their way from the Perumal Temple in Serangoon Road to the Chettiar temple in Tank Road.[19] He remained unaware of his caste till his marriage in 1966 (he was 49 then), when he accidentally stumbled on the fact. Was such lack of awareness because of the Self-Respect Movement and the sermonising by Ramasamy Naicker on the evils of the caste system? Had the ancient system lost all relevance? But then a basic awareness of the caste dividing lines had not absolutely vanished, past experiences of abasement and rejection continued to rankle. Undeniably, the essence of the caste system — the hierarchy and the endogamy, had persisted and continued to influence their lives. But then why such ignorance on Bala's part?

 Perhaps it was part of an unconscious lack of identification with such practice. He was unintentionally setting aside festivals and traditions with which he could find little in common. Part of it was the colonised Asian's stereotypical lack of connection with his roots — when Shakespeare and Scott intervened in his understanding of ethnic rites and systems. But part of it was perhaps the fact that Tamil religious practice in Singapore was largely shaped by the first migrants — the labourers. It was a spiritual practice which pivoted around the worship of localised village gods or *gram devatas* like Mariamman or Vairavar or Muniandy — gods who would protect rural communities from disease, pestilence and natural calamities. Thus the Sri Mariamman Temple of South Bridge Road, the oldest Hindu temple of Singapore, built by the first Indian to set foot here — Naraina Pillai. A tradesman from Penang, he suffered immense loss when a fire destroyed his business in 1822. And then when he could revive his business with the assistance of Raffles, he built a temple — a small wood and *attap* structure — dedicated to Mariamman, the goddess of rain and a guardian against small pox. Again the Veeramakaliamman Temple on Serangoon Road, flanked by Belilios Lane to which Bala was a frequent visitor. Built around 15 years after the Mariamman Temple, its residing deity is Kali, a goddess who needed to be placated to avoid calamity, a less benevolent version of Durga, who is said to reside in the cremation ground and who is worshipped on the dark, moonless night of Deepavali. The Veeramakaliamman Temple right from its inception was associated with the many Indian labourers of Serangoon Road and that this association continued till much later is evident in a news which appeared in the *Singapore Free Press & Mercantile Advertiser* (1884–1942) on 8th December 1936: 300 Chinese skilled artisans working in the River Valley Works of United Engineering Ltd had joined forces with the 1,300 Indian workers (employed by the Municipality, the Civil Aerodram etc) who were already on strike in demand for higher wages. In light of the above, G Muruthamuthoo, Trustee of the Veeramakaliamman Temple had made the following appeal to the public:

> "The Veeramakaliamman Temple at Serangoon Road, opposite Veerasamy Road has been maintained all along by the labourers of Singapore. In consequence of the present strike many destitute have surrendered to the temple. About 5,000 people are being fed twice daily. All generous-hearted are earnestly requested to give their help to this deserving cause. Donations of any nature, however small, will be gratefully accepted at the temple."

For Bala, visiting the temple would have been quite a thrilling adventure. In his early childhood he may have been witness to animal sacrifice and though such sacrifices were banned in the early 1930s, the *balipitam* or sacrificial altar remained. As did the central shrine of Periyacci — a goddess to whom new mothers offered food to avoid any calamity befalling their children. He would see devotees in *arul*, a trance-like state when they sang and danced in a frenzy. He was witness to the famous fire-walking festival, Timithi, which in actuality is a re-enactment of the rape of Draupadi. During the build-up to the festival, devotees enacted scenes from the *Mahabharata* — Draupadi's modesty being outraged, her vow to leave her hair open till she could smear it with Duhsasana's blood, the sacrifice of Aravan, Arjuna's son to appease Kaliamman and then the actual battle of Kurukshetra with the final fire-walking ritual symbolising Draupadi walking through fire to testify her purity. Or the Thaipusam festival when worshippers in an act of penance thrust sharp skewers through their tongue. While as a boy Bala would accept with glee the *prasadam* offered by the temple priest, later he would marvel at the depth of religious fervour of the worshippers and the strength of their faith which made such acts of self-atonement possible. But perhaps simultaneously there remained an element of disconnect which prevented him from ever indulging in such acts of salvation himself. And perhaps consequently, in his adult life he unconsciously veered towards the neo-Hinduism Movement of Singapore with its emphasis on a greater institutionalisation of Vedanta-Hinduism and involving a certain urbanisation or secularisation of religion.

Conclusion

What emerges out of Bala's boyhood or youth is at best an amorphous miasma of emotions, an equivocal jumble of rather muted likes and equally feeble dislikes. If sports and literature were emerging as passions, they were nipped in the bud as he busied himself with learning the first skills of commerce — typewriting and shorthand. In his future life, sport would mean cycling down to office and literature would be reduced to a copy of the Omar Khayyam which still resides on his bedside table. The little windows to the outer world which his reading was opening up were quickly closed as first his family was faced with the aftermath of the slump and then the period of Japanese Occupation approached — more formidable in its privations than the Great Depression. Yet the first flush of tenderness he had felt for his favourite Shakespearean heroine, Portia, remained and he would marry a woman who most definitely combines the qualities of empathy and an effective, pragmatic acumen. His dislikes too could be measured against a similar scale of ambiguity — if he had little to celebrate in his own boyhood, living as they did on meagre resources, he never expressed it even to himself and yet through his life worked hard to provide his family with a better life. If he felt a sense of discord with the religious praxis of his mother, it never struck him to protest. Instead, in his adult life he gravitated towards a more individualistic and enhanced form of Hinduism.

For a migrant in any part of the world, the first markers of identity are perhaps his village or the hometown from which he hails, his caste, his ancestors or the extended family, and the religious community to which he belongs. These are the elements which colour and contour his character. Yet Bala was virtually ignorant of the first three and felt little affinity for the last. Thus his individual character did not evolve out of these founding pillars. Instead, he allowed himself to float, suspended plankton-like in midstream, as time buffed and polished his personality, much as it did to his country, Singapore. It is only gradually that he learnt to trust his instincts and accept his capabilities. He learnt early though the first thumb rule of migration — survival of the fittest — and this social Darwinism kept him going. He adapted, evolved, learnt new skills and kept himself afloat, not allowing the green algae to close over him. And it is this migrant's willingness to reinvent himself which allowed him a niche in Singapore, even as the country emerged from a febrile blankness to discover its own unique identity.

When he was in school Bala would delight in Shakespeare's lines, "Why should a man whose blood is warm within/ Sit like his grandsire cut in alabaster,/Sleep when he wakes, and creep into the jaundice…" He would recite them when alone with an unaccustomed, portentous lift to his voice. The rest of his life would be spent in comprehending why the lines had given him such pleasure.

Notes

[1] *Lorong (M)* = narrow, winding alleyways

[2] *Vaanam (T)* = sky, *Langit (M)* = sky

[3] *Veshti (T)* = *dhoti* or lower garment typically worn by Indian men

[4] *Kai vaithiyar (T)* = traditional doctor

[5] *Potong (M)* = cut, here used in context of cutting a kite

[6] The river has since been narrowed and some of its water channelled elsewhere.

[7] *Pasir (M)* = sand

[8] *Chandu (M)* = opium

[9] *Dhoby (H)* = washer man

[10] *A History of Modern Singapore 1819–2005*, C M Turnbull. NUS Press, Singapore, 2009.

[11] *Pottu (T)* = the dot worn at the centre of forehead

[12] Details of old Singapore from: *Travellers' Tales of Old Singapore*, Compiled by Michael Wise, Times Book International, Singapore, 1985.

[13] *Lascar (H)* = East Indian sailor, *Jamban (M)* = rubber receptacle used in toilets

[14] *Singapore's Little India: Past, Present & Future,* Sharon Siddique & Nirmala Puru Shotam. ISEAS, Singapore, 1990, p.33.

[15] The menagerie was later shifted to a 27-acre plot in Punggol and was the predecessor to the Singapore Zoological Gardens.

[16] The Singapore Traction Company (STC) started the service of trolley buses on 14 August 1926. Before this both steam and electric trams had plied the roads, but the operations were gradually wound up by 1927 because of the inconvenience of maintaining the tracks.

[17] *Kolam (T)*=A design drawn with rice flour; *Murukku (T)* = a savoury snack made of rice and lentil flour.

[18] *Samfu (C)* = the Chinese trouser suit

[19] *Kavadi (T)* = devotees carry a *kavadi* during Thaipusam. It consists of either pots of milk slung on a pole or two semi-circular pieces of wood or steel that are attached to a cross structure that can be balanced on the shoulders of a devotee. The *kavadis* are known for their decoration of flowers and peacock feather.

Circa 1932. A family portrait. Bala stands with his sister Chandra Bai on his right. His mother Rajambal is seated, holding his sister Sulochana. Photo taken at a studio on Selegie Road.

CHAPTER 2

Nothing without Labour

Pre-War Post Office Days: 1935–1942

"We felt but did not grasp that truth,
Until the years, the changing age,
Confirmed severely: Nothing without
Labour; nothing is for free.
You grew us well, Mother of our youth,
…We shared ourselves, and found ourselves
…here our better youth
Was spent, that we were salted then. We
Do not return to you. We never really left."

Victoria School, Jalan Besar, Singapore
— Edwin Thumboo

The Twelve Apostles

"The British rolled through town in limousines, lived in sumptuous villas and revelled at exclusive clubs while the rest of the Asiatic population starved, toiled and died."[1] Thus wrote a Japanese journalist of the *Singapore Herald* with a touch of righteous disapproval of the colonialists of Singapore in the late 1930s. He was a columnist for a propaganda broadsheet and possibly played his role in convincing Japanese authorities back home that time was ripe for an attack. He described with some relish the life of indolence the British led with their domestic needs taken care of by an Indian houseboy, a Malay driver and a Chinese *amah;* the officers who rolled into office in their luxury sedans at 9 or 10, lunched at 1 and retired to the club with a gin bitter by 5 in the evening. In short, it was deemed as a life of futile aimlessness which needed immediate correction.

Without such scathing criticism, life in Singapore did have a touch of complacence in the mid-1930s. The British administration ran on well-oiled wheels with a seemingly indifferent population of immigrant communities, intent eventually on returning to their home countries and so happy to leave matters of governance to the colonial authorities. Public amenities had improved and the rich and the educated led lives of reasonable comfort.

But underneath the epicurean lifestyle, tectonic plates were in motion, forming new patterns and connections, preparing for the storm that was to come. One of the starting points of such change was the Great Depression of the 1930s, after which, as Turnbull said, the British Empire never really regained its zest and vitality. While the Empire lost some of its vigour, the depression left in its wake an Indian community where close to half the population of immigrant workers lost their jobs. There was a resultant mass exodus of Indians from the FMS to Singapore in search of a living. Such privation brought with it an attendant sense of resentment and a will to fight for worker rights and amenities. There would be a marked increase of trade union awareness in the community in the pre-war period and this would neatly dovetail with the rousing Indian nationalism of the INA (Indian National Army) Movement of the 1940s.

So what was it that triggered the Depression — was it a debt conversion that lowered interest rates, was it too many risky investments of the past which eventually caught up, a bad harvest, the end of a war? Possibly it was the normal cycle of overtrading in stock markets, followed by revulsion and discredit, leading to credit being cut off to internationally traded commodities, a plunge in commodity pricing leading to debt-default, capital-flight and a widening circle of financial disaster. But such intricacies of economics were not for Murugasu and his family. All they knew was that Murugasu's work had been on the wane for a while, essential commodities were getting dearer and their first born, able-bodied son was coming of age. Consequently, when Bala passed his London Chamber of Commerce Examination at the close of 1935, it was decided without much ado that he should start looking for a job.

Bala, if asked if he wanted to study further, pursue literature perhaps, says with his usual calm pragmatism that he knew that to be impossible. Instead he registered his name with the Students' Employment Service of the Education Department and sought employment through personal references as well. His first attempt was to get the job of a male nurse with Tan Tock Seng Hospital, the greatly refurbished Pauper's Hospital which in 1909 had moved from Serangoon Road to Moulmein Road. In 1930 the hospital had set up brand new x-ray facilities which had greatly benefited citizens, but it had also been in the news for yet another, more sinister reason — suicide attempts among patients. As the hospital grew more stringent about cleanliness and restricted movement of patients with communicable diseases, some took recourse to desperate measures.

Bala continued on his search for a job. Like in his student days, caution marked his life — he looked for safe jobs which needed skills of book-keeping and typewriting. Without a viable role model in his community, a middling clerk's job in a government-owned enterprise seemed the maximum he could aspire for. It was at this time that a former classmate, Shanmugam, took him to meet one Mr Kanesan, a clerical officer at the General Post Office (GPO). Unfortunately, there was a bit of subterfuge required at this early stage: Kanesan claimed Bala was his nephew and so vouched for his integrity to get him an interview appointment.

The day of the interview dawned. Bala cycled down from his home in Serangoon Road to the Fullerton Building (the National Heritage Board, Singapore gazetted the Fullerton Building, now the Fullerton Hotel, as Singapore's 71st National Monument in December 2015) on the banks of the Singapore River which housed the GPO. He was to meet B Neyland, the Assistant Controller of Post. Fortunately, Neyland turned out to be one of those British men of many past-times so despised by the Japanese columnist of the *Singapore Herald*. He was in the news as much for his work in the post office as for the Sepoy Lines Golf Championship he had won (1934) and the annual picnic he organised for the post office employees at Tanjong Rhu (1937). It was the same Bert Neyland who would discover a rare talent for drawing cartoons in the years to come and would publish a regular feature in the *Singapore Free Press* titled *Army Laughs*. And subsequently, when interned for three years during Japanese Occupation, he would continue to draw cartoons on the back of prison forms and these later would be exhibited as wartime memorabilia.

On that day he quizzed Bala on the England and Australia Test Games and the forthcoming Ashes and was impressed by his achievements in school sports. Though the interview went off well, Bala left with a faint sense of misgiving as he had been unable to answer Neyland when he pointed to a painting of a ship on the wall and asked him to which company it belonged. Possibly, Neyland's indication was to a steam ship of the Royal Mail Steam Packet Co. which in 1932 had been taken over by the newly formed Royal Mail Lines. The latter ran an extensive pattern of interlocking marine routes and was the owner of a large fleet of beautiful white and gold steamships which plied the waters around the world for the conveyance of mails.

But despite the worry, in due course he received a missive from the postal department of Singapore that he had been selected. The event was occasion for some celebration and his mother took him to the Mariamman Temple, thanking the goddess for saving the family from further hardships.

On the appointed date, Bala presented himself at the office of B J Freeman. He realised he was to be a part of a 12-man unit, a group of Malay, Indian and Chinese boys who had been recruited along with him. Neyland escorted them to the room of Freeman, the Controller of Posts & Telegraphs, Singapore. He also had been the Justice of Peace for Singapore since 1934 and the boys were invited to take a solemn oath of integrity and diligence to the P & T Services in front of him. It was a grave ceremony at the end of which Neyland declared they were his specially selected group of 12 apostles, champions who would uphold public confidence in the P & T Department. Indeed, it would be the first year when the postal department organised such large-scale recruitment of trainee clerks. For Bala, as it turned out, it would be a journey of 35 years.

When Bala joined on 1st July 1936, the postal department of Singapore had a clearly distinctive presence from the rest of Malaya. In 1935 the silver jubilee of King George V had been celebrated, postage stamps carried his vignette and for an airmail to travel between Malaya to Great Britain a flat rate of 25 cents per 1/2oz for letters and 15 cents per postcard would be charged. Direct airmail service between Europe and Singapore had been introduced in 1933 and the journey took approximately 13 days including both directions while in 1937 international calls between Singapore and London via radio-telephone were introduced with a three-minute call costing $51 and the service being available from 4.50 pm onwards daily at the GPO.[2] Incidentally, the Straits Settlements (SS) had introduced its first official postcards in 1897 and for the next 15 years these postcards enjoyed the special rate of 3 cents for international distribution and only 1 cent for use within SS and the Malay States. Privately printed pictorial cards were also in prevalence and as early as in 1898, postcards depicting local scenes and special events of Singapore, with space for a private message along the bottom or the sides of the picture, had made their first appearance and had subsequently gained in popularity.

Early 1937 saw the opening of the post office at the Changi RAF base and the closing down for renovations of the Kampong Glam post office. Thus, Bala was entering a busy world which was evolving fast and changing daily. It had its own set of rules and regulations with which Bala would have to make an early acquaintance. During his long career he would often find himself taking on new and challenging job assignments, decisions which would help him in the future.

History in Pigeon Holes[3]

Bala started work as a probationary clerk from 1 July 1936, an appointment which was renewed on a monthly basis till he was duly confirmed on 1 March 1937. During the first year he was trained at the various branches of the postal department and found himself spending considerable amount of time in the Mails Branch of the GPO.

The Fullerton, one of Singapore's most imposing buildings, had been completed in 1928. Built at a considerable cost of $4.75 million, it boasted quite a few of the features for which colonial architecture all over Asia is justifiably famed — a distinctive frontage with Doric columns, the double-volume, first storey GPO Hall with a full-coiffured ceiling and full-length windows, strategically placed air wells through which natural light flooded in (remodelled as the atriums of Fullerton Hotel) and a traditional timbre fenestration. In his speech marking the inauguration of the GPO on 27th June, Sir Hugh Clifford drew attention to the building's magnificence and interestingly, mentioned one of the very areas where Bala would spend considerable periods of time — the sorting office in the mails branch: "The sorting office is a masterpiece in itself. Situated at the bottom of one of the areas [the first level above the basement], it is roofed in glass, set in a reinforced concrete roof. The roof has a 48-foot span, the construction of which was no mean achievement considering the type of labour that was required." Though impressive, the description is slightly marred by what came just before it: a description of a system of small-windowed watching galleries which had been built near the ceiling, high up in the walls from where a supervisor could keep vigil on the workers below without himself being observed. The ceiling was made of opaque glass which allowed enough sunlight to flood in while cutting out some of the tropical heat and it was in this environment of strict vigilance that Bala stepped in, proving himself from month to month as he learnt the various steps involved in having a letter reach its designated destination: first, the letters which came in collection bags from all over the island and were emptied into a large trough, here the letters were picked up for cancellation of stamps by hand stamping and by the stamp cancellation machines. Afterwards the letters were carried by trollies to a central sorting section where Bala and his peers placed them in the 48 pigeon holes of the sorting frame and thereafter the letters were conveyed by manually pushed trolleys to the dispatch section. According to Bala, the work was hard because he had to be on his feet the whole day, moving around the sorting area, but at the same time he found it stimulating — country names and foreign streets bringing to mind pictures of a world he was yet to see.

He also worked in the Telegraph Branch where he learnt to send and receive Morse code messages, a skill that would come to his rescue during the forthcoming war. Sir Clifford in speaking of the telegraph room had mentioned the compressed air tubes which connected the telegraph room with the telegraph counter and through which messages were sent. The telegraph room was also connected to a wireless room on the roof which worked on the short wave system. Yet another startling discovery for Bala was the underground walkway which snaked out from the GPO's basement which was several feet below high water mark and was otherwise used for parcel sorting and strong-rooms. Underground tunnels for the conveyance of mails featured in other parts of the Empire as well as in London as a means of lessening on-road congestion. In Singapore it travelled below Fullerton Road and out to the post office pier on the beach. The part of the GPO building abutting on the seafront was taken up by the Master Attendant's office and the Marine Court and hence the pier often went by the name of the Master Attendant's Pier.

The mail destined for the neighbouring countries of Southeast Asia were picked up from the sorting room and conveyed by a spiral chute to the basement below from where trolleys stacked high with mail bags were pushed to the end of the tunnel and brought by a lift up to the pier level. Till July 1939 the mail-loading platform was on a pontoon which rose and fell with the tide. But afterwards an electric platform was installed which could be adjusted to suit the height of the tide and the pontoon was shifted to the airport. At the Master Attendant's Pier, Marine Department launches waited which would ferry the mail bags to the ships harboured at the outer roads beyond the Clifford Pier. The ships would be mostly small, privately owned vessels which travelled to the neighbouring countries. On the other hand, the mail bound for Europe and beyond was carried in GPO vans to the Tanjong Pagar docks where P & O Company ships were harboured at the wharf in preparation for the long journey. Bala speaks of monthly Mail Notices which were published by the GPO in Singapore newspapers. The notices were detailed lists of ships departing Singapore with corresponding times of posting at the GPO for letters intended for such vessels. Customers, particularly commercial firms would time the dispatch of their overseas correspondence accordingly. A vessel could depart the Singapore waters only after the post office had advised the Master Attendant of its acceptance of mail. The closing of mails was signified by the Master Attendant by flying a flag from the Fort Canning Signal Station. Interestingly, till the 19th century a red ensign signified mails to Europe while a yellow one was for China and the arrival of mails by night was announced with a round of gun fire from the fort. Bala remembers that an announcement that a British ship was in port would often happen on a Friday and that would mean a very large number of mail bags being conveyed to the GPO and the sorting clerks working hard and extra time, at times on Saturdays, to clear the large quantity of mail and so have it ready for expeditious delivery. But this was before the war and before the formation of any postal union and so, according to service conditions, there would be no overtime payment for the extra time worked.

Unknown to him perhaps at that time, Bala was fortunate to have joined the Singapore postal department, a postal and communication hub for the entire Southeast Asian region since Singapore's inception as a trading post in 1819. The novelist Joseph Conrad went to the extent of describing the GPO of Singapore as the most important post office in the East. Given Singapore's unique position at the crossroads of international sea-routes, it continued to be the collecting and forwarding hub of all mails for the region till the late 1800s when neighbouring countries became members of the Universal Postal Union (UPU) and so could receive and send international mail. Till before this, for example, Straits Settlements stamps were merely overprinted with a 'B' and used in Bangkok. But even subsequently, with the opening of the Singapore-Kranji Railway in 1903, Singapore would become the terminus of an extensive railway system spreading through the Malay Peninsula and Thailand and so continue as an important port of call.

In fact, the first post office of Singapore was established as early as in 1854, on the bank of Singapore River, a spot accessible only by boat. It was in 1856 that a footbridge was erected and a toll of a quarter of a cent levied. By 1873, the post office was shifted across the Singapore River to be on the same bank as the Commercial Square (or today's Raffles Place) and renamed the General Post Office (GPO). This new location at the site of the former Fort Fullerton proved to be far more accessible for traders and merchants and the building was later demolished to make way for the much more impressive Fullerton Building in 1921. The Chinese Post Office Riots of December 1876 form an important landmark in the history of postal service when Chinese *towkays* rose in protest against the building of a Chinese sub-post office at 81, Market Street, a British agency established with the express purpose of collecting and forwarding all China-bound letters and remittances.[4]

The amount remitted by Chinese immigrants was estimated to be an annual 50,000 Spanish dollars at that time, an amount big enough for rivalling parties to stake their claim on it. The riot mobilised by a Chinese secret society was however soon quelled by the British and the Chinese postal business absorbed into the mainstream. However, the system of having a Chinese Package Service for mails delivered from and to China by postal agents who had been licensed by the GPO would continue till much later.

It was in 1926 that it was decided that there was need to coordinate the functioning of the postal department of the Straits Settlements with that of the FMS and a joint headquarter was established in Kuala Lumpur. The post offices of the SS were merged with P & T, FMS to report to the Director General of Posts and Telegraphs of Malaya, a position held by T P Coe, at the time of Bala's joining, while Singapore was headed by the Controller of Posts and Telegraphs. With the transfer of the headquarters to Malaya, the Singapore postal district came under the charge of a Controller, a position held by B J Freeman at the time of Bala's joining. With the increase of business in Singapore, suburban and district sub-post offices were opened. As early as in 1897, the first three sub-post offices were opened outside the commercial area in Kandang Kerbau, Tanjong Pagar and Tanglin and by the time of Bala's joining in 1936 there were as many as 17 sub-post offices and six postal agencies on Singapore Island alone and the horse-drawn mail coaches had been replaced by motorised vans. Besides, the success of a series of experimental flights saw the establishment of the first direct air-link with Europe in May 1933 by the KLM Royal Dutch Airlines. This was quickly followed by Imperial Airways in December, which inaugurated a regular airmail service between London and Singapore. Thus, in 1933 Singapore was made the airport of call for east-bound and west-bound flights of KLM which provided airmail service not only to Europe but to the neighbouring Palembang and Batavia as well. This meant by 1935/36 a letter from England would take six to eight days to reach Singapore which in August 1845 would have taken 41 days when the first P&O (Peninsula & Oriental) steam vessel, Mary Wood brought mail via the Suez to Singapore. Incidentally, the speed of postal delivery would receive a further boost with the introduction of jet aircrafts in 1952 — airmails from London now arrived within 48 hours after posting by the BOAC (British Overseas Airways Corporation) Comet Jet Service.

Interestingly, the first stamps to be sold at the Singapore Post Office were the imperforated lithograph stamps of India. This was in 1854/1855 and consisted of four values – half anna, one anna, two annas and four annas. These were soon followed by the perforated stamps of the East India Company and when in 1867, the seat of the government of the Straits Settlement was moved to Singapore, the same East India Company stamps were overprinted with a crown and surcharged at 3&1/2 to 32 cents. Thus, initially letters sent from the Straits Settlements of Singapore, Penang and Malacca used the same Indian stamps while numbers were assigned to distinguish between the letters sent out from the three settlements: 'B172' for Singapore, 'B109' for Malacca and 'B147' for Penang while 'B' stood for Bengal since the Straits Settlements were under the supervision of the government of Bengal in India. Later at the beginning of the 20th century, stamps would carry King Edward's head in vignette with a coconut palm as an emblem of Singapore, a betel-nut palm as a symbol of Penang and sugar cane (*gula melaka*) as that of Malacca.

A Stool for the Gentleman

According to the *Straits Times*, by early 1938, the 10th birth anniversary of the Fullerton Building, there was a staff of five Europeans and 700 Asians who handled over 200,000 articles each day at the GPO. The counter in the main hall remained open till six in the evening and saw a steady flow of customers the entire day.

During the latter part of Bala's probation, he found his way to the central counter, the pride of the post office. Built in solid wood panelling with chest-high grilles separating the staff from customers, the counter was 300 feet long. It faced the main entrance, curving around to the Fullerton Road frontage and was reputed to be the longest post office counter in the British Commonwealth. It was at the counter that for the first time trainees like Bala had a stool assigned to them on which they could sit and conduct the day's business. Since it involved interfacing with customers, Bala had to dress neatly and wear a tie to complete the picture. He soon realised the racial hierarchy he had witnessed outside was in prevalence here too — English customers were to be treated with particular courtesy, more so than the locals. Normally, the English just ambled up to the counter and expected to be served first while others stood aside without much ado. However, as earlier when he had been witness to racial differences, this incident too did not breed any resentment in Bala. He merely took it in his stride as part of the natural order of things.

The part of the training that he enjoyed the most was manning the Poste Restante counter. Tucked away in one corner of the long central counter, Poste Restante was particularly useful to travellers who did not have postal addresses where their letters could be forwarded. Instead they simply addressed their letters "c/o Poste Restante" and such letters would be held by the post office till the recipient called for them. Bala enjoyed hearing the travellers' tales while he processed the letters, a rare indication from his youth of an urge to break free, a wander lust, a call of adventure which continued to lure him.

At the end of the probation period, the trainees were assigned to different departments. Bala, with his exceptionally good scores in the Morse code tests, found himself in the Telegraph Branch of the GPO. The Singapore Telegraph Office had been opened in 1909 with public lines functioning between Singapore, Kuala Lumpur and Penang. Though telegraphic services were opened to the public only in 1909 with the central telegraph office as well as telegraphs installed at the sub-post offices, Singapore had been linked to KL and Penang by electric telegraphic cable as early as in 1859. By the end of 1917 Morse Sounder Quadruplex instruments had been installed between Singapore and KL. Initially rather primitive single-needle machines were used which by 1926 had given way to the Wheatstone System in which holes corresponding to the Morse code was punched into a paper slip using a hand-machine. This was of course to be transposed onto a telegraph form at the receiving end. Here the Creed printer came in handy, a machine where the process was reversed and the punched paper when passed through the machine produced a paper tape with the typewritten transposition ready for the lay reader. Bala spent considerable amount of time sending and receiving telegraph messages by not only using the Morse code tapping instrument but also tele printers which made use of telegraphic waves to connect the tele printers at the sending and receiving ends so that when a key corresponding to a particular character was pressed at the home station, it activated the typewheel at the distant station and the same character was printed at the receiving end. Hours of work in the department were long with the telegraph counter open around the clock but it was an important technical skill which would auger well for Bala in his future career.

As a part of his training, Bala also learnt to handle the public telephone service offered to customers. Private phones were not unavailable in Singapore. In fact one Bennett Pell, manager of the Eastern Extension Telegraph Co., had given Singapore a head start as the first colony in the East to have a private telephone exchange a mere three years after Graham Bell patented his invention. The central telephone exchange was on Hill Street and by 1937 international call facilities were also made available. Yet, rental rates for residential phones were high and consequently telephone call facilities were made available to the public at the GPO as well as some of the sub-post offices. Under it a person requiring to make a call would make a request at the post office counter and pay in advance the call fees of 10 cents for a three-minute call. The counter clerk would dial the requested number and while the customer spoke at the nearby telephone booth, would closely monitor the conversation so that he did not overstep the time limit. Conversations normally tended to exceed the time limit and Bala did not savour the duty of interrupting the flow to switch off the line. An inherent sense of propriety intervened and he felt compelled to apologise to the customer before he could bring himself to disconnect the line.

Around this time an opportunity presented itself. The Controller of Posts, Mr Freeman, advertised for a position in the newly established

Southern Division Engineering Branch at the GPO. Members of the staff were welcome to apply. With the expansion of the telephone services and the development of other forms of telecommunication, there was need for a specialised department devoted to engineering at the GPO which would be entrusted with extending the telegraphic lines, adding new routes and laying the underground wires. Bala responded to the circular and with his experience in handling telegraphic communication and Morse code machines, he was selected for the position. He was made in charge of the staff attached to the engineering branches of Singapore, Malacca and Negri Sembilan, a challenging position which demanded both administrative skills and technical expertise. Earlier in the year he had been sent for short stints to three sub-post offices. The first was at the Kandang Kerbau sub-post office, which, established in 1897, was one of the earliest sub-post offices and was located at the western end of Serangoon Road, on the banks of the Rochor Canal. The name Kandang Kerbau (later shortened to KK as in KK Hospital), meaning *buffalo pens* in Malay, referred to the many slaughter houses which operated in the area till the 1920s and the post office catered to the large Indian populace of the vicinity. Later, he had worked at the Queen Street branch which was essentially part of a British enclave and then at the Kampong Glam sub-post office, an area inhabited largely by the immigrant Muslim population of Singapore, i.e., the Malays, Arabs, the Javanese and the maritime people of the Bugis community. This kind of a rounded exposure to the multi-racial communal life of Singapore combined with the new experience he would glean in the engineering division would eventually make for an enviable foundation to Bala's future career in the posts.

A Dream and a Nightmare

"On the day the sun shines with the moon
Our arrow leaves the bow
It carries my spirit towards the enemy

> *With me are a hundred million souls*
> *My people from the East*
> *On this day when the moon*
> *And the sun*
> *Both shine."*

Thus wrote Tomoyuki Yamashita, Tojo's contemporary and in all probability Japan's most able general, as he sailed to invade Malaya with his hurriedly assembled army. But even as war clouds were gathering at the horizon, Bala was living some of the happiest days he had known since childhood. For the first time life seemed full of hope. Work at the post office was not easy but he enjoyed interacting with people, learning new skills and moreover there now stretched in front of him a tangible pathway to success which he could scale with his efforts. For the first time the controls were in his hands and for Bala this sense was gratifying.

As he cycled his way each morning from his residence at Rappa Terrace to the GPO, he would often find himself whistling a tune. It was pleasurable to dream of the future — a future when he might become the post master of a sub-post office. Earlier, while posted at the Kandang Kerbau Post Office he had seen the lifestyle of the post master. He had rent-free quarters atop the post office where he lived with his family and even possessed a car. To the 21-year-old Bala it seemed like an enchanted life, a life truly worth striving for.

Unknown to him the brief interim of happiness was going to be very rudely disrupted. Before he knew it, it was December 1941 and Pearl Harbour had fallen. During the next few months, as Japan rapidly overtook vast tracts of territory in Hong Kong, Malaya, Burma, Thailand and the Dutch East Indies, and units of the British Army flooded Singapore giving it the look of a garrison town, his life would change forever. Like all generations that have lived through war, he would never again take for granted any happiness that came his way, his only abiding faith being in the transience of life.

In early 1942 he was taken off his regular duty at the engineers' office and instead mobilised to serve the Fortress Signals Company of the British Army. In fact, even earlier, while attached to the Telegraph Department he had been encouraged to enlist as volunteer in the Signals Company. He had joined eagerly as it gave him a chance to brush up his Morse code skills. Part of this decision to have him join the volunteer force was of course because of his past experience in the Telegraph and Engineering Divisions and part of it was also continuation of Churchill's intention to concentrate naval strength in Europe and depend on local mobilisation of forces for the protection of the East. While the British Admiralty promised that the protection of Singapore, Australia and New Zealand would take precedence, till end of 1939 the assumption remained that a fleet would be dispatched to Singapore in the event of an attack. In the meantime, while the King George VI dry dock was inaugurated and the eastern approach to the naval base in Changi reinforced, journalists continued to hail Singapore as the *Gibraltar of the East.*

The Royal Corps of Signals, a support arm to the British Army, had been established in 1920. Always the first to swing into action during war, the Corps of Signals provided the information and telecommunication infrastructure that was necessary for an army to function. Between 1920 and 1941, the Royal Corps of Signals had spread its wings to the Far East and as the war situation deteriorated it comprised several signal sections, including the Malaya Command Signal Company with its offshoot, the Penang Signal Section as well as the Singapore Fortress Signals which eventually Bala joined and which was formed of local personnel in 1938.

Bala soon found himself at the Signal Company's camp which was at first located close to the St Patrick's School campus on East Coast Road. Interestingly, as was customary in units of the British Army, he found here too racial divides were rigorously maintained — there were separate dormitory huts for the Europeans and Eurasians, another for the Chinese and a third for Indians and Malays. Meals were also eaten in separate mess rooms.

Life at the camp proved to be quite a life-changing experience for Bala. Among his camp mates was his postal colleague, G Kandasamy.[5] Younger than him by four years, this young man from Penang had joined the postal services in 1937, a year after Bala and worked in a clerical position at the GPO. Later, he would rise to the position of Assistant Controller of Posts but would decide to give it up and instead join politics as a member of the People's Action Party and emerge as one of the foremost trade unionists of Singapore. Camp life would bring the two together and subsequently, Kandasamy would work closely with Bala for the Singapore Union of Postal and Telecommunication Workers when it was formed in 1946.

At the camp it so transpired that on an occasion men from the Indian section protested because of the poor quality of food being served. They decided to boycott the morning breakfast. The commanding officer was disturbed but after discussing matters with the Army HQ, he managed to have the food rationing improved though Bala and his mates had to contribute a small amount from their service allowance to the mess fund for maintaining the quality of the food supplied. This proved to be an important life-lesson for Bala — firstly, henceforth he would know that it was all right to protest, all that was unfair did not have to be accepted with a resigned calm as part of one's destiny and secondly, that negotiations, when rationally conducted, could actually lead to improvement in life's amenities.

As the Japanese Army moved southwards down the Malay Peninsula, the camp site moved first to the campus of the Chinese High School along Bukit Timah Road and subsequently, to the Beach Road military camp opposite Raffles Hotel which was the headquarters for the Singapore Volunteer Corps (the first Singapore Infantry Regiment consisting of 22 privates of the 1st Battalion would be raised at the same site). Bala and his mates maintained a strict routine with morning parades, route marches and rifle range practice. But as part of the Signals Corps, the major focus of their work remained on telecommunications — running radio and area networks, laying temporary lines and exchanges and Morse code testing.

During the final days of his assignment with the Signals Corps, he was scheduled for duty at the Grange Road Listening Post, conveyed daily to and from the Beach Road military camp in an army truck. In the meantime the Japanese blitzkrieg in Singapore had continued with the British steadily losing the initiative. Singapore was bombed on the night of 7th/8th December 1941 and within 24 hours Japanese troops landed in Thailand, with ancillary landings at Sungei Patani and Kota Bharu: air control was lost, the naval base was nearly empty and the army was the sole survivor, bearing the brunt of the campaign. Yet despite the carnage, local life continued with the nightly dances at Raffles Hotel and the New World Cabaret still open. Evacuations had started by January but the desperate scramble was yet to begin. Thus, it came as no mean surprise to Bala when on the 15th of February 1942, he received a High Command telegram sent by his friend Kandasamy from Fort Canning stating that General Percival, the commander of the Allied Army, had surrendered and all service men were to remain at their posts until further orders.

Bala at the time of receiving the message was at the Grange Road Listening Post while Kandasamy would have been in the Signals Room of Fort Canning where the Singapore Fortress Signals was headquartered and in charge of internal communications (while Command Signals was responsible for communications in and out of Singapore). The Signals Room, which many called the 'post office', was where messages were picked up or sent off, manned by seven men per shift: three signal men, two orderlies and two clerks. The message would have been received by the Signals Operator, via wireless or from the cables and once decoded it would have been handed over to the Signal Officer for onward forwarding. Kandasamy, aware of the full import of the message, followed it up with a telephone call so Bala was left in no doubt.

Bala felt deeply shocked. Japanese brutalities were not unknown to him and his colleagues and they wondered what was to be done next. After some consultation they decided to escape. The British Officer-in-Charge very kindly agreed to turn a blind eye to their impending disappearance and the men hurriedly took off their uniforms and boots.

So, within an hour of receiving the telegram, Bala found himself on the road, barefoot, stripped down to his singlet and underwear. He did not know where to head; whether it was safe to go back home or what had happened to his family. It was as if he had completed a full circle and was as vulnerable and defenceless as he used to be when he would run after falling kites by the banks of the Rochor River shouting, "Potong! Potong! Potong!"

Only he felt much less hopeful.

Conclusion

Bala would eventually find his family with the help of his friends from the Indian Youth League (IYL). He had joined the IYL in 1939 during the early days of his work life, a year after the League was established by young, English-speaking professionals from the Indian community with the prominent solicitor S C Goho as President and Dr K R Menon, then a teacher from a private school, as Secretary. The offices of the IYL were housed in a rented property in Race Course Road and its members were mostly from the Tamil working class, besides some professionals and businessmen from the Indian community. Bala's primary involvement with the League was in the sports field and as member of the Management Committee, he even encouraged the youth to take up boxing! However, the League's primary sports focus was football and they managed to engage in friendly games with other clubs. Around the beginning of the 1940s it came to Bala's attention that the Negeri Sembilan Football Association was organising a Bharden Memorial Trophy for Indian clubs and he, as member of the League decided to apply for the IYL team to play in the tournament as a team representing Singapore. It was the first time that a Singapore team had participated in the trophy. The journey did not stop there — the Singapore IYL team managed to secure a narrow victory in a well-contested semi-final match played in Farrer Park against the team from Malacca. Subsequently, the victorious team travelled to Seremban to play the final match in the Indian Association premises against the

Selangor Indian Association team. Unfortunately they lost the match but at least a beginning had been made.

This association with the League is a remarkable incident from the short six years of Bala's work life during the pre-war period. Before his involvement with the League, as a younger boy he had participated in some friendly football matches organised by the Tamil Brotherhood Party but never experienced the pleasures of voluntarily taking up a leadership role.[6] Besides, while in his childhood, under the influence of his parents, he had imbibed Indian traditions, that was more of a subliminal assimilation, involving very little conscious thought or voluntary action. But now, once he got to know of the League through a network of Indian friends, it was a deliberate decision to join the body. And then during the turbulent days of war and Japanese Occupation when he received considerable help from League members, for the first time he felt a sense of gratefulness, a stab of loyalty to not only the League but to the community he belonged. Being an Indian became a more conscious part of his identity, a consciousness which would be further sharpened and fine-tuned under the influence of Netaji Subhas Chandra Bose and the INA.

This short six-year period from 1936 to 1942 is also remarkable because it saw Bala emerging from the chrysalis of a parent-imposed cautious and often anodyne existence, a chary, below-the-radar lifestyle which they preferred and considered safe in a foreign land. With his new job at the post office and his initial success, Bala had a first taste of confidence. And subsequently, with the incident regarding food rations at the Signal Company's camp, he felt an all-new sense of fulfilment in being able to achieve a tangible benefit for himself and his peers.

This new-found confidence and a new awakening to the wrongs of a racially divided society would later urge him to work for the Singapore Postal Union. And the same confidence when combined with a heightened awareness of his Indian roots, would motivate him in reform efforts for his own community. In the late 1930s there were two movements which influenced the Indian community of Singapore — the first was a carryover of the trade unionism triggered by the Great Depression. In Singapore it brought to the forefront leaders like S C Goho (Srish Chandra Goho, who also spearheaded the IYL) and K P K Menon — lawyers who played a key role in the strikes of the Singapore Traction Co. of 1938 and the Klang Valley strikes of 1941 when Goho took a pro-active role in demanding better wages and living conditions for Indian labourers. The second was a continuation of the Dravidian Movement of the 1920s which saw the establishment of the Tamils' Reform Association (TRA) in 1932 — a body meant for collectively presenting Tamil demands to the British but more importantly, aimed towards reviving the lost glory of the Tamil culture. The paper *Tamil Murasu* became the movement's mouthpiece and large-scale plays were staged to present Tamil culture while Tamil education and the establishment of Tamil medium schools were actively propagated. Bala, during his lifetime (with some important exceptions) would find himself straddling both the movements, though as he is fond of saying with self-deprecating humour, only as a team member, never as a leader.

Bala's family reminiscences of the particular care with which he handled every official issue which came up for his decision making. Even when at a considerably senior position, he would stop to weigh all possible options and attempt to view the problem from all possible perspectives before he took a decision. Rarely if ever would he take an impromptu decision based on insufficient data. Why did he feel the need of such consistent diligence? Perhaps this is an indication of the kind of value he attached to his postal work. Arguably, it was his work which had given him hope in an otherwise dismal situation. It was the caliper scale of meritocracy that every migrant searches for — a calibration against which he proves himself daily and justifies to himself his right to stake a claim in the new land. The period of 1936–42 is remarkable because it provided him with such a scale and also because it saw him take on a number of roles. It saw him grow from a boy to a man, a dependent to a breadwinner, a clerk in a Sorting Room to a young official with considerable administrative responsibilities, from a bystander of selfish dreams to an up-stander on an active lookout for a mission.

Notes

1. The quotation is by Tatsuki Fuji of the *Singapore Herald*.

2. Postal trivia from *Malayan Postal History to 1939 as Recorded in Official Documents*, compiled by William Arnold Reeves. Malayan Study Group, London, 1984.

3. History of Singapore postal service from newspapers like the *Straits Times, Singapore Free Press & Mercantile Advertiser* and *Singapore Chronicle*.

4. *Towkay (C)* = businessmen

5. Bala while at the Signal Company's camp also met Dr Goh Keng Swee who became Singapore's first finance minister.

6. Bala became a member of the Tamil Brotherhood Party (TBP) which organised football games amongst the Tamil youth and was initially located in a garage in Rangoon Road. He recalls the Secretary, S R P Naidu, was a civil servant and encouraged Bala as well as others from the team to play football. They would practise in the Farrer Park race course grounds, without any coaches and more often than not without football boots. They participated in a tournament organised by the Singapore Indian Association. After the war TBP renamed itself the Tamil Brotherhood Association, had an office in the Farrer Park Sports Complex and Bala became a trustee. Though the TBA continued to encourage the Tamil youth in sports, interest waned and subsequently the Association existed in a moribund state.

Postcard from before 1936. A scene from the perspective of Anderson Bridge. Sampans seen are from the Singapore River, where it meets the sea. The small building to the extreme left was the water boat house — here the provision of fresh water for the ships was organised.

Fullerton Building taken by Kelly & Walsh Ltd, printer/publisher, Raffles Place, Singapore.

1939. Bala (standing, left) and the Tamil Brotherhood Party football team participating in a match, probably at the Singapore Indian Association.

CHAPTER 3

**How You Wrestled Nippon-go
Far into the Night**

Japanese Occupation: 1942–1945

"They return, those walks before the sun grew hot
Along broken, morose roads skirting the Japanese Camp,
Passing rusty bren gun carriers retreating Brits forgot.
Day 3-9-5 into the war you counted…
How you wrestled Nippon-go far into the night,
Moving up from guttural roots, nursery rhymes…
To teach to feed us. Precarious job. Kept despite
The hard, deep-gripping consonants that maimed
An English-crusted tongue unwilling to be tamed."

Father — IV, Singapore
— Edwin Thumboo

Fall of Singapore

On 15th February 1942, when Bala stepped out of the Grange Road Listening Post, the first thought that struck him about the city was how silent it had all become. It was the hushed silence of a graveyard. There were no pedestrians on the roads, shops were shuttered. News of the pillage and slaughter which the Japanese military had unleashed in Malaya had travelled to Singapore and all civilians preferred to stay indoors. The landscape too looked surreal. There were open craters in the roads, columns of smoke rose from bombed sites, cars and trolley buses lay abandoned, their pantographs having been uprooted from overhead wires. There were rotting carcasses lying on roads and a strong smell of explosives in the air. Orchard Road and Chinatown had seen the worst of the bombing and the many shophouses of the city had proven to be veritable death-traps. Even on the 14th the *Straits Times* had bravely declared that Singapore would stand firm — a promise that had obviously proven to be an empty one. The Japanese had landed in Thailand on 8 December 1941, within 10 days they had taken Penang, were at Kuala Lumpur by 12th January and by the end of the month in Johor Bahru, facing Singapore across the waters — a progress of around nine miles a day which had taken everybody by surprise.

Writing about the day a year later, the Japanese newspaper *Syonan Sinbun* would comment that only Dante could have described the last days of Singapore in 1942. Autobiographies from the time carry different memories. Lee Kuan Yew writes of the Sutherland Highlanders who played on their bagpipes even as the last of them crossed the Causeway and the Royal Engineers blew open a gap on the Johor side. The sight would leave him with a lasting impression of British equanimity in the face of defeat. Jumabhoy, who along with S C Goho had been helping Indians to evacuate, had already left for India on 4th February. He writes of leaving most of his household furniture and belongings with a friend in Scotts Road. But on his return after the Japanese surrendered he received only a few pieces of his monogrammed crockery — the Japanese had apparently plundered his friend's bungalow during the initial days of the occupation. Maurice Baker, like many others, writes of his sense of complete surprise. As a citizen of a British colony, he and his peers were immunised from the possibility of British defeat, not very long ago having been enthralled by stories of the brilliant British evacuation of half a million soldiers from Dunkirk. Even when overthrown the English were perceived to be heroic. They had been brought up on English history and continued to believe that the British might lose a battle or two but that the final victory would be theirs.

On the 15th, Bala initially took shelter with Ponnampalam, a friend who lived in the staff quarters of the General Hospital at Sepoy Lines. He spent two restless days there and on the third day he left Ponnampalam's residence and walked the five miles to his home in Rappa Terrace. There he was finally reunited with his family who had been evacuated by his friends from the Indian Youth League (IYL) to a rubber estate in the Seletar Hills. Bala remembers two things from the time — the warm welcome he received from his mother and from his friends from the IYL once he reached home and his own relief in the knowledge that he carried in his pocket the two months' advance salary payment which his English boss had given him just a few days before the Japanese had come. There would be no immediate dearth of money.

Bala's connection with the core team of the IYL would remain, despite the various stages of evolution the association went through. As a member of the IYL, he would be involved in organising sports activities for the INA in and around Race Course Road. During the time of Japanese invasion, the IYL, led by S C Goho, played a key role in aiding Indian evacuees. They helped put together the Indian Passive Defence Force and the 800 odd volunteers worked at relief camps which provided food and shelter to Indian refugees forced to flee their homes. In fact, Srish Chandra Goho or S C Goho, a Bengali from Calcutta, was a person of some importance in Singapore's Indian community. He had been politically active since 1935 and in 1940 had been elected the President of the Singapore Indian Association. He would prove to be a dynamic leader with the membership of the League growing manifold soon after its inception, and his politics would take direction from political movements in the Indian subcontinent. Consequently, the IYL would consistently gravitate towards the Indian National Congress, advocate Indian nationalism, celebrate Gandhiji's birthday (and denounce his incarceration) and in 1943, break away from the Rash Behari Bose-led Indian Independence League (IIL), because its leaders felt Bose was brokering the Indian nationalist cause to the Japanese.[1] Bala's pre-war friendship with members of the IYL would mean he too would be influenced by their thinking. During the critical years of the Japanese Occupation he remained committed to the cause of India's independence at all cost and even distanced himself from the Tamils' Reform Association (TRA) because he felt it was more inclined towards a particular community and not moving in tandem with the Indian National Congress.

Resumption of Work

It is typical of Bala's nature that he feels grateful to both the vanquished British and the victorious Japanese: to the first for the two months of salary advance they gave him which protected his family from immediate starvation, and to the second because they accepted him back into the postal service. And so it transpired that he continued to work at the GPO without much to disrupt his career graph, serving the job-in-hand rather than the current nationality of his supervisor. But one does wonder if this apparent objectivity was merely his superior work ethic or the compulsions of survival? Maybe it was a combination of both plus the fact that the Indian community continued to be one of the most transient ones in Singapore, feeling itself to be a fleeting presence, even more so than the two other major communities, the Chinese and the Malays, who also incidentally continued to gravitate towards their own kind. As Turnbull observes, when the Japanese arrived, unlike in Burma for instance, there was no sense of Malayan nationalism which they could exploit. As far as the Indians were concerned, they carried firm intentions of returning to India in the future, an emotional predilection which would gradually change only after the bloodbath which followed partition. Bala remembers that while posted at the Kandang Kerbau sub-post office in the pre-war years, Indians formed the majority community in repatriating money, often taking help from petition writers available at the GPO to send money back to their homes. Their livelihood in Singapore was merely a conduit to ultimately achieve a better life back in India. Perhaps this is why there was such a fervent response to Subhas Chandra Bose's INA Movement in Malaya — a struggle for an independent India gave them hope of return. This was also a reason for the popularity at this time of movements like the IYL which nested within the Indian nationalist movement rather than the TRA, which emphasised socio-cultural reform. Indian independence remained more relevant to the future of the expat community and, as in other colonised countries, the urge for freedom inadvertently slowed down reform.

Whatever the cause may be, in Bala's case, this objective view of his job as a means rather than an end afforded him a certain efficiency and a typical migrant's advantage. He found he could appreciate the work ethics of the Japanese as much as he had that of his English bosses. Within a fortnight of their arrival, the Japanese Military Administration began to revive some of the public service departments. During the first week, employees of the waterworks, electricity board and the Municipal Corporation were called back to duty and by 1st March clinics and dispensaries were reopened. The first *Shonan Times* (the *Straits Times* renamed, renamed again in December 1942 as *Syonan Sinbun*) appeared on 20th February, proudly proclaiming the apparently altruistic aim of the Japanese in establishing the East Asia Co-Prosperity Sphere meant for achieving a "great spirit of cosmocrasy". And in less than a month the newspaper was describing the 16th of March, the first month anniversary of Nippon administration, as the first day when "civilians woke up in peace" with electricity and water services revived.

Bala found himself to be one of the few members of the P & T staff to be re-employed for work in the GPO. In the initial days of the Occupation, a few senior English postal officials were released from internment camps and allowed full access to the records of the P & T Department. This was to facilitate the restoration of the services as the Japanese invasion had not only disrupted the postal services but had also led to considerable confusion as the naval commanders fleeing Fort Canning ordered the burning of naval cypher books (and perhaps even the code books) which prevented the reading of coded signals from approaching ships.[2] But apparently, the English officials used the period of free access to destroy records of those like Bala who had been volunteers in the British army. This act of unselfish munificence, for which Bala remains grateful, protected him from the wrath of the Japanese and consequently, even as the Chinese community of the city faced the horrifying *sook ching* purge and decapitated heads of looters were prominently displayed in street corners, he found himself re-ensconced in the Singapore GPO. On 16th March the *Shonan Times* would write of the reopening of the postal services, describing the "pleasant spectacle of seeing Malay and Chinese postmen dressed in their unmistakeable khaki uniform" delivering letters again to the citizens of Syonan. Thus, the GPO as well as the sub-post offices of Geylang, Kampong Glam, Keppel Harbour, Newton, North Canal Road, Orchard Road, Paya Lebar, Queen Street, Sepoy Lines, Serangoon Road and Tanglin would be reopened on 16th March 1942, postal rates would remain unchanged and the self-congratulatory tone of Japanese propaganda would continue as newspapers reported of the population of Syonan now provided with facilities to speedily contact friends with whom they had lost touch during the "dark days of mid-February".[3] Incidentally, it was during this period that Singapore would see its first pictorial stamps: the Japanese would hold a stamp design contest and five of the designs with an emphatically Asian motif would be selected and issued in 1943 as 1-, 2-, 3-, 4- and 8-cent stamps.

At the Kakugo Gakko

Bala resumed work in the Mails Branch of the GPO under quite a changed set of circumstances. The Japanese army had been handling the mail during the initial days of the occupation till civilian services were organised. Postal communication to Singapore from several of the Malayan states too had been disrupted since the British had blown up the east coast railway at multiple points and could be resumed only in mid-June 1942, once the necessary repairs had taken place. Though the postal rates remained the same, stamps issued by the Straits Settlements now needed to be overwritten with a red Japanese chop, and a new mail service from Japan to Malaya was started with rates similar to the domestic ones. Pre-war Straits Settlements stamps were overprinted across the portrait of King George VI so as to deface the portrait of the sovereign head of the British Empire. Initially, the stamps were hurriedly overprinted by hand with the Malayan Military Department's seal, while later, they were overprinted by machine with the words "Dai-Nippon-2602-Malaya" (i.e., Greater Japan Postage) and by 1943, *kanji* characters on the stamps were replaced with English ones. Another area of change was the postal arrangements which needed to be made for the vast number of POWs and internees held in the gaols of Singapore and Malaya. Communication with the Allied countries was resumed only after 17th June 1942 and by then, there were about 250,000 POWs assembled in camps around Singapore. At one point of time at the Changi Internment Camp alone, there were prisoners of 41 different nationalities. Although a Prisoner of War Bureau of Record and Enquiry was established in Changi towards the end of 1941, a Bureau that was responsible for not only the sorting of POW mails but also tracking down the POWs themselves, censorship continued to be intense. Besides, the Japanese government continued to contravene several regulations of the Geneva Convention meant for fair treatment of POWs and consequently, the issue of postal service for POWs remained a prickly one, with rules being amended frequently and several instruction booklets circulated by the postal department to clarify doubts. While in the beginning, letters and postcards were merely to bear the words, 'Prisoners of War Post', by end 1943, letters to civilian internees in Japanese-occupied territories were to be limited to 25 words with an alleged intention of speeding up censorship.

The Japanese Occupation period remains memorable to Bala for the rare pleasure he found in learning Japanese, particularly the ideogram-based Chinese characters or *kanji*.[4] He surprised himself by the keen interest he took in learning the language, first enrolling himself for the primary course in learning *katakana* and *hiragana* and then moving on to the more advanced course in *kanji*.[5] He would eventually graduate from the *Kotoka* or Advanced class with distinction. This was despite the difficulties of the time which proved to be one of the most trying for most Singaporeans, not only because of the menacing presence of the Japanese *Kempeitai* (military police), but also because of the very real problem of food supplies running out and the plummeting value of the *banana* money.[6] Though a guild association, or *kumiai*, was established, essential commodities remained in short supply and a thriving black market sent prices soaring.[7] This was a time when Lee Kuan Yew's mother made ends meet by baking cakes from sago flour and selling them, and similarly, in other households the enterprising skills of house wives were stretched to limits as various alternate resources were tried, including grinding egg shells in place of calcium pills. Consequently, the Japanese ran a Grow Your Own Food campaign, farming became a part of the school syllabus and the Owen Road end of Farrer Park was neatly fenced off and given to vegetable farming. As the *Syonan Sinbun* of February 1943 brazenly wrote, while children played, parents could make use of their time by tilling the soil.

In the beginning Bala joined the *Syonan Nippon Gakuen*, the first Nippon-Go (Japanese language) organisation of the Japanese Propaganda Department. In all probability, he was a part of the first batch of 400 students when the school started on 1st May 1942, completing the first term in July the same year and then moving on to the second and third terms with the advanced course limited to the graduates of the school. Subsequently, after October 1942, the school would be handed over to the Education Department of the Military Administration and renamed the *Gunseikan-bu Kokugo Gakko*, located at Queen Street.[8] On 30th October 1942, on the occasion of the closing down of the *Syonan Nippon Gakuen*, Professor Zimbo, principal of the school, would address the graduating students.[9] The ceremony would be held at the Dai Toa Gekijo (the Cathay Theatre renamed) and the elderly professor would explain the reasons for establishing the school, reasons which throw some light on the situation of the time. The first reason, like most Japanese decisions, was utilitarian — he had taken on the responsibility merely because the Military Administration had no time for education-related interventions during the busy days after war. But the second reason is perhaps more interesting — *to search for the cultural tendencies of the citizens of this new territory.* The professor had obviously had a tough time assimilating the kaleidoscopic mix of races and languages that Singapore presented, the likes of which he had never seen in "Nippon homeland". But he had persisted, fully intent on bringing unity to the "chaos and confusion" and so instituted the Flag Hoisting Day on the 8th of every month, the Naval Day and other important days. He felt such joint celebration of important days on the Japanese calendar had helped in bringing some order to the chaos. As his third reason, the professor cites the need to teach the citizens the Nippon-Go language as well as introduce them to the Nippon spirit so they could know more about the Nippon-zin, or, a Japanese person.

Bala had a satisfying experience at the *Nippon Gakuen* and still has fond memories of the teachers — if not as individuals, as a dedicated group who earnestly tried to share with them aspects of the Japanese culture. Professor Zimbo in his speech mentioned Masatake Oyama, a teacher who also wrote a book of Japanese conversation for use in the school as well as Lance Corporal Tsugio Kunitani from the Higher Normal School in Hiroshima who had compiled yet another textbook. In fact, Kunitani would continue to teach at the *Kokugo Gakko* of Queen Street and during Bala's time there would become the school's principal.

On 30th October Professor Zimbo had ended his speech with a touching line: "Goodbye *Syonan Nippon Gakuen*! Your recollections [will] be beautiful forever in my bosom!" There is a simple earnestness in these lines, a quality to which Bala would respond repeatedly in his interactions with the Japanese, be it in his postal work or at the Japanese Language School. At the *Gunseikan-bu Kokugo Gakko* of Queen Street too he would be touched by the teachers' sincere efforts to explain the Japanese way of life to students. Here he would interact with teachers, quite a few of whom were graduates from Japanese universities who had taught at the Singapore Japanese School in Short Street during the colonial period. In 1941, when the war started, the British Army had closed the school and several of the teachers had been interned in India as POWs. They had returned to Singapore only in 1942 under an agreed POW exchange programme and Bala was impressed by their endearing love for their own culture and country, despite the vicissitudes of war. Perhaps this affected him more because so far in his 25–26 years of life he had had little opportunity to experience any passion for his country — be it India or Singapore. His sense of patriotic loyalties would be stirred for the first time by Subhas Chandra Bose's INA Movement and even then he, like many other second generation Indians in Malaya, would feed off the nationalist energies of the Japanese.

In focusing on the positive face of Japanese nationalism, Bala perhaps decided to make the best of a rather trying situation. If there is a lack of critical engagement with its negative aspects — the parochial and restrictive urges — then maybe it can be excused as the compulsions of survival. As under the British rule, with the Japanese too he decided to ignore the tell-tale signs of unfairness and disparity, and continued with his life as best as he could. Though arguably, the signs were many and hard to ignore. For instance, on 21st February 1942, i.e., within six days of British surrender, the *Syonan Times* explained the meaning of the term "Syonan" — it referred to "Syowa", the contemporary era of Nippon history. Thus, the new name of Singapore was in effect a commemoration of the Nippon people, a celebration of the Yamamoto race and though the same article also proclaims Nippon's intentions of giving "all coloured or Asiatic people peace and glory", as it would turn out, the "glory" could be achieved solely by merging with the Nippon culture. And the Nippon-Go language would become the chief vehicle for disseminating this Nippon-zin culture. The newspapers of the subsequent months bear testimony to the rigorous efforts to make Nippon-Go the *lingua franca* of Japanese-occupied Asia: there are daily lessons in Japanese words and grammar, translations of Japanese nursery rhymes which can be used by new mothers, children's columns which speak enticingly of the *Hinamatsuri* festival of dolls, articles on the *bushido* spirit which inculcates sacrifice and moral strength, and musical scores of Japanese marching tunes which can be sung by the Asiatic people to celebrate their new-found freedom.[10] There are veiled threats in stories of fathers who know only English and Malay and who are advised that it might be useful for their children to pick up Nippon-Go so they could secure better jobs later.[11] There are carefully laid baits as well: the *kanji* characters came from China many years ago and since more than 50% of the population of Syonan was Chinese, it was all the more in the fitness of things that Nippon-Go should be adopted. By June 1942 the tone becomes more dictatorial; since there was no possibility of the British returning, it was imperative that every doctor, lawyer, secretary or clerk should learn the language if they wanted success in their careers or any kind of government favours. All the while the underlying message remains clear — the Nippon culture was a superior one, the Nippon-zin having been educational peers of the ancient Greeks, and if Western culture was to be eliminated and replaced by the higher, nobler civilisation of Nippon, the entire Asian race needed to cooperate in learning Nippon-Go, for the Nippon-zin spirit could only be expressed in Nippon-Go. Or as Professor Zimbo said on 4th August 1942, in a ceremony celebrating the first batch of students who had completed the primary level of learning, of which Bala would have been a part, "Behind Nippon is a long history of 3,000 years which reveals the eternal and untiring efforts of the Nippon race. You have just made your first step on this old mountain….I hope all of you will be good Nippon-zin…you will begin to understand the high qualities of Nippon culture in the course of learning about Nippon."[12]

Bala graduated from the school at Queen Street, which was arguably the most successful of the Japanese language schools in

Singapore. Incidentally, even Lee Kuan Yew went to the same school, as a part of the first batch of 1942, and writes in his memoirs that he found Japanese easier to master than Mandarin because the former was not tonal, though more complicated in its inflections and grammar. For Bala, learning the language and achieving good grades meant he was transferred from the Mails Branch at GPO to the *Yusei Kyoku Somuka*, i.e., the Staff and General Affairs Branch of the postal headquarters, and assigned the duty of looking after postal employees who arrived from Malaya (renamed *Malai*) and Sumatra for training at the Queen Street *Kokugo Gakko*. The postal training scheme started in the beginning of 1943 with the first graduation ceremony of second term students being organised on 16th June 1943. The trainees were lodged in postal quarters at Battery Road and walked to and fro from there to Queen Street. The initiative was driven by the Education Department as well as the Director General of Posts, with the trainees not only learning Nippon-Go but also receiving instructions on the Nippon system of postal work. Occasionally, entertainment events or a *Post Office Night* would be organised with the programme consisting of the showing of Nippon movies at the Dai Toa Gekijo and the Syonan Broadcasting Station Orchestra rendering a selection of musical pieces.[13]

During his training at the *Kokugo Gakko* as well as afterwards, Bala would try hard to remain focussed on the ingrained qualities of the Nippon-zin. He would come away impressed by not only the sense of nationalism but also their respect for elders and devotion to duty. As he watched them taking on multiple roles — military officials who did vegetable farming as a part of their duties, or his teacher Kunitani who along with his army duties was the principal of the Queen Street *Kokugo Gakko*, he would be convinced that given the right attitude and dedication, anything was possible and achievable. Such idealism would remain with him for life as would his love for the *kanji* characters — an artistic form of self-expression which he continued to practice even at an advanced age.

A Stranger in the Crescent

Bala barely knew about Subhas Chandra Bose when the leader landed at Sabang, an isolated islet off the coast of Sumatra on 6th May 1943. In comparison, Nehru was a more recognised name, particularly after Pandit Jawaharlal Nehru's visit to Singapore in May 1937. Bala had of course heard of Bose, both from his father and his friend, P Ranga from the IYL, but had little inkling that his arrival would change his own life in different ways — for the good and maybe even for the not so good.[14] In a reversal of the butterfly effect, the momentous event of a famous Indian nationalist arriving in Southeast Asia would continue to produce small, nonlinear changes in Bala's life for many years to come — in fact, few from his community would remain unaffected.

Murugasu had heard of Subhas Chandra Bose before, though for him Gandhiji and Pandit Nehru were more representative of the Indian political scene. At the time of his leaving Thanjavur, though the Indian National Congress was the dominant political party, there was a prominent presence of the Madras Mahajana Sabha as well in the South, a party older than the Congress by one year and with popular leaders like P Rangaiah Naidu, G Subramania Iyer and C J Mudaliar. At the turn of the century the Seventh Madras Provincial Conference of the Madras Mahajana Sabha had been held at Kumbakonam, the town in Thanjavur from where Murugasu hailed. In fact, at the time of his leaving India, Bose would not have been a part of the political scene at all, having been born in 1897, and having left for Great Britain in 1919 to study at Cambridge and sit for the qualifying exam of the Indian Civil Service. Thus, his name could not have been a familiar one in the household, not really a name Bala grew up with. Instead, it would have floated into his consciousness only around June 1943 when the Japanese newspapers as well as INA's *Azad Hind* paper started active propaganda in favour of Bose, though possibly Bala would have heard some of the open broadcasts made by the leader from Berlin since the fall of Singapore in 1942. Till then, Bose had been living incognito in Germany, after having dramatically escaped British clutches in

January 1941. It was only with the fall of Singapore and the turn in Axis prospects that he came back into view and his countrymen heard his familiar voice once again, "This is Subhas Chandra Bose speaking to you over the Azad Hind [Free India] Radio."

Regular articles on Bose started appearing in the *Syonan Sinbun* around June 1943. Thus, on 15th June, D B Sehe, the president of the Philippines branch of the Indian Independence League (the civilian-administrative body attached to the Indian National Army, INA, which spearheaded the Indian nationalist struggle in Southeast Asia, of which Bose would soon be the leader) would write that all India had lacked was a militant leader and now with the arrival of Subhas Chandra Bose, determined to cooperate with Nippon in routing out Anglo-Americans from India, the long years of patient suffering by Gandhi would finally bear fruit and India's independence would be within easy reach. Such write ups which effectively connected the diasporic movement with the indigenous one was reinforced by articles denouncing the British and their malevolent treatment of Gandhi and Nehru and was particularly aimed at swinging the opinion of the Indian civilian population in East Asia in favour of the Japanese.[15] If this was not enough to dispel doubts about the essential dissonance between Gandhi's Civil Disobedience Movement and the armed resistance towards which the INA was moving or the news that the subcontinent as a British colony had entered war on the side of the Allies, there was additional information on food shortages in India due to British hoarding and on an impending famine, which unfortunately would turn out to be a bitter reality.

Thus the ground had already been prepared by the Nippon radio and print media. Like a farmer preparing soil for planting, the first layer of earth and loam had already been placed in convincing the Indian community that time was indeed ripe to join the Indian nationalist struggle with the aid of the Japanese. Added to this was the Nippon-zin spirit which many like Bala had imbibed since the beginning of the occupation — their sense of intense nationalism and earnest industriousness. The impact of such a culture was there for all to see in the first flush of Japanese victories against the apparently invincible Anglo-American powers round the world. It was a time when the Japanese slogan of *Asia for the Asians* was popular and the prospect of building a Greater East Asia Co-prosperity Sphere seemed a feasible one. Bala too was in a somewhat alert mental state by June 1943. His friends had told him about Subhas Chandra Bose and his sacrificial patriotism and he had been reading newspaper reports regularly: when M Sivaram, the editor of the *Azad Hind* paper wrote that the presence of Bose at such a short flight distance from the frontier of India could mean only one thing, *Action, Action, Action,* or when Rash Behari Bose, the elderly nationalist who was about to hand over the baton of IIL to Subhas Chandra Bose described him as one who symbolises all that is best, noblest, daring and dynamic in the youth of India.[16] Yet, by his own admission, nothing could have prepared him for the prospect of physically witnessing Subhas Chandra Bose.

The 5th of July 1943 started as any other hot summer day in Singapore. As the morning progressed, the sky became increasingly overcast and heavy with the promise of rain. Bala, along with a couple of friends from the IYL, walked from his home to the large open field in front of the Tokubetsu Shi Building (Municipal Building, today's City Hall, renovated as the National Galleries) at the Singapore Esplanade. He found that a large audience had already gathered and he could see many familiar Indian faces in the crowd. Not only civilians, there were also present large detachments of smartly attired soldiers from the Indian National Army. As the clock tower at the Victoria Memorial Hall struck the hour, the cavalcade carrying Subhas Chandra Bose rolled in. To everyone's surprise, he was not wearing a *sherwani* — the Indian long coat that everybody expected. Instead, he was dressed in a soldier's greens with top boots and a peak cap. A steady drizzle started and Bala watched from where he was standing near the Cenotaph in Connaught Drive. The *Padang* was virtually full with Indian soldiers and a huge multitude of civilians, and the Cenotaph proved to be a better spot from where he could watch as Bose refused the umbrella that was proffered to him. The bugle sounded, the troops presented arms and Bose was led by senior Japanese officials, the INA Army Chief and the senior leader, Rash Behari Bose, to inspect the army. Then he ascended the flight of stairs to the Corinthian colonnade and the dais that awaited him. From the rostrum, Bose could see the serried ranks of Indian soldiers, and he started his address: "Today is the proudest day of my life. Today, it has pleased Providence to give me the unique privilege and honour of announcing to the whole world that India's Army of Liberation has come into being." He spoke in English and Hindustani which was later translated into Tamil by M K Chidambaram of the IIL.

Bala would later wonder why a stranger from Bengal, a part of India of which he had very little awareness, had such an impact on him. As he walked back home with the surging crowd he felt as if fireworks were still bursting in his mind. He felt numbed, incapable of thought, with the rousing words still ringing in his ears. The world around him, the snarling afternoon traffic, the hooters and the hackney carriages seemed to have receded, too mundane to even take into serious consideration. His mind kept going back to the last words: "For the present, I can offer you nothing except hunger, thirst, privation, forced marches and death. But if you follow me in life and death — as I am confident you will — I shall lead you to victory and freedom. It does not matter who among us will live to see India free. It is enough that India shall be free and that we shall give our all to make her free." As he ended, there had been a moment of pin-drop silence, so silent that Bala had felt he could hear the gentle lapping of water against the stone sea-wall. And then the thunderous applause broke out. As the air was ripped by cries of *Inquilab Zindabad! Azad Hind Zindabad!* (Long live the revolution, Long live free India), Bala had felt shaken to the core. He felt the prick of unshed tears behind his eyes and he found that involuntarily, his hands had balled themselves into fists.

Why did the incident affect him so intensely? Was it because for the first time, when Bose declared the INA's war cry, "To Delhi, to Delhi", Bala could actually close his eyes and visualise India — the *Lal Kila* or Red Fort of ancient Delhi and the victory parade of Indian soldiers in front it — the high walls and ramparts, the fortification with extended hornworks and the columns of battle-hardened soldiers marching three abreast with the captain ahead of them, holding up the Indian tricolour? Was it because Bose seemed to bring India closer, to make it more real, and Bala had felt an instant connection? Or was it because it was the first time he had witnessed an Indian of such stature, speaking with pride and confidence, and the sight had filled him with an unfamiliar longing — a need to identify with such a display of dignified valour? Or was it just Bose himself? His steady candour, firm voice, the way every cell, nerve and sinew of his body seemed to be drawn together in voicing his conviction?

Unfortunately, Bala would not be able to surrender to this great tidal wave of emotion which had welled up within him. Murugasu's usual pragmatism and caution would come in the way of his joining the INA or the IIL. However, Murugasu would send his elder daughter Chandra Bai, who had come of age, to join the Rani Jhansi Regiment (RJR). She would live mostly on camp at the RJR site, close to the intersection of Bras Basah and Victoria Street, near St Joseph's Institution (where the Singapore Management University stands today), coming home occasionally during weekends. The younger daughter Sulochana, who was still a minor, would join the *Balika Sena* (Youth Wing) and go to the Ramakrishna Mission compound at Norris Road for regular parade practice and singing rehearsals. Bala would continue with his job at the GPO and would soon find that it had been a propitious decision for the family.

Though Bala did not join the INA, a lingering sense of purpose remained with him as did a certain excitement at the thought that they, as a part of the migrant community, could play a role in shaping society and as change agents. It was this sense, underscored by a heightened awareness of the unfairness of British rule generated by the Japanese, which would come to his aid in the post-war years. The INA went on to score some major victories in the initial period after Bose arrived, the chief among them being the great upsurge of response the movement managed to evoke among the local community.

In fact, the response was so overwhelming that by 13th July (8 days after Bose's speech at the *Padang*), the recruitment department of the IIL was turning away prospective applicants. Though this initial euphoria did not last and there was no dearth of naysayers as the INA, defeated and greatly depleted, straggled back from Burma, a certain fond admiration for Bose remained in the Southeast Asian crescent, particularly in Malaya. And this proved to be one period when among the Tamil migrant community, the Indian nationalist movement enjoyed more prominence than the Dravidian Self-Respect Movement greatly popularised by Ramasamy Naicker (also named E V Ramasamy Periyar) since the 1930s. Part of this was of course due to the INA's alliance with the Japanese, which lent it legitimacy, but part of it was also perhaps the essentially inclusive nature of the movement. Right from the outset, Bose's speeches were translated into Tamil, the INA's former flag had carried the emblem of the striped tiger in remembrance of Tipu Sultan, and his speeches held references to the Vellore Mutiny against the East India Company, engineered by the brave son of Mysore from the southern part of India.[17] The Dravidian Movement which had sought to restore the self-respect of non-Brahmins had differed little from the aims of the Justice Party of India, led by Periyar himself, and for some time the primary political alternative to the Congress in Madras. The Justice Party had remained at odds with the Brahmin-dominated Congress and with Gandhi because of his alleged praise for *Brahminism* and at one point even demanded that the southern states secede from the subcontinent to form an independent *Dravida Nadu*. The INA, with its emphasis on communal sensitivities, perhaps could side-step this Dravidian-Aryan conflict which had raged for years. For the egalitarianism attempted by the INA was different from the unity preached by the Japanese — it did not entail submerging individual identities in a "superior Nippon-zin" culture but was born of a joint celebration of communal differences and cultures. Another reason of conflict between the Justice Party or the earlier Madras Mahajana Sabha and the Congress had been social reform, particularly in the context of women and the caste system. The former emphatically believed that before nationalism swept away all other priorities there was need for radical restructuring of the traditional Hindu society, while Congress remained divided on the issue. But perhaps this urge for social reform nurtured by the Dravidian Movement in Malaya was also somewhat met by the INA with its lack of adherence to caste structures, communal kitchens and gender parity as represented by the Rani of Jhansi Regiment. Thus, there were certain elements in the INA Movement which dovetailed with the groundwork already done by the Dravidian Self-Respect Movement and this perhaps helped the former in reaching out all the more effectively to the Tamil community of Southeast Asia.

A Departure

As it has been famously written, it was the best of times, it was the worst of times, it was the age of wisdom, it was the age of foolishness, it was the spring of hope, it was the winter of despair — that was the kind of mixed bag of legacies that the INA Movement left in Bala's life. On one hand just as it stirred his emotions and left him with a lasting sense of mission, for his family the period also remained associated with a deep personal tragedy.

Around the time the INA Movement started gathering steam and the first rumours of Subhas Bose's arrival to Southeast Asia floated in, the Japanese also started conscripting men of working age for military-related work projects. This included not only POWs from the British-Indian Army who had refused to throw in their lot with the INA, then led by Captain Mohan Singh, an ex-soldier of the 14th Punjab Regiment, but also civilians. But it was in March 1943 and with the possibility of an Allied attack in Burma that the Japanese accelerated their projects and consequently, the number of recruitments, particularly of civilians, also rose significantly. Thus men from Malaya would find themselves building airstrips on the distant islands of the Dutch East Indies or working in the mines of Japan. But the majority of them would be pressed into work on railway projects in

Thailand, Burma and Sumatra. The recruitment cycle would typically begin with the Japanese 7th Army of Thailand and Burma passing an order to its counterpart, the 29th Army of Malaya, who in turn would pass it on to the Malayan Labour Department to fill the required quota of men. The Labour Department which during the British times had recruited mostly plantation labour would then swing into action and, using the services of agencies which included branches of the IIL and the Chinese Association, would track down workers.

Thus, though it is not known for certain, there is a possibility that Murugasu heard of the Thai-Burma Railway project at the office of the IIL. At this time, the IIL branches had become quite the central meeting point for the Indian community, the Japanese having entrusted the League with a plethora of administrative work including population registration, making of ration cards, etc. For the Railway Project, the Labour Department promised almost $15 a month, slightly more than the pre-war rate of around $14 per month for similar work along with free transport to the work site, free accommodation and even the possibility of travelling with family. It was said the contract would be an open one for three to six months with a promise that workers could return once the project was completed.[18] It is true that Murugasu, already in his 50s, would have seen little prospect for his English speaking skills or his work as an itinerant trader in the Japanese occupied Singapore. Prices of essential commodities had been soaring and there was a serious problem of food shortage with the Japanese Army's policy of stockpiling reserves. Murugasu could have heard of the Thai-Burma Railway project with interest with its prospect of a guaranteed income coupled with the possibility of food allowances for the family. But nothing prepared him or his family for what happened next — Murugasu disappeared around July 1943. It was only later that the family got to know that he had been conscripted for the project. According to reports, the first tranche of Labour Department-sourced workers left Kuala Lumpur in April 1943 and similar freight wagons, each carrying a couple of hundred men, women and children herded together, would continue to leave for northern Thailand and Burma over the next few months. July would prove to be the peak month for the Labour Department when, as per records, as many as 7,815 labourers were sent in 12 separate batches.

Such civilian conscripted labour or the *romusha* suffered perhaps an even worse fate than the POWs who at least had a support structure and some leadership. The exact number of *romushas* used on the railways is not known, though the highest figure is estimated at 270,000. Murugasu could have formed a part of the predominantly Tamil group which was sent from Malaya to Thailand, possibly to the Kanchanaburi Camp. It is not known under what circumstances he was brought there or he worked. The Japanese authority had permitted a limited amount of mail facilities for the civilian labourers and set up postal service in some of the districts of Thailand including Kanchanaburi for this purpose. Yet, Bala's family never received any news from Murugasu. They merely heard that the railway had been completed in October 1943 but that the men had been retained, and of the dismal living conditions in the *romusha* camps where men, with little idea of hygiene or contagious disease, died like flies. They heard that the dead were often left where they fell, adding to the spread of disease.

Thus, Rajambal and her children never got to know what befell Murugasu — whether it was the deadly cholera or malaria or beri beri or just fatigue. They never knew what kind of work he had been assigned to do — stone quarrying or cutting down jungle or carrying heavy wooden sleepers through hostile forests. They never knew when or where he died or whether at that time he harboured any dreams of ever returning to Thanjavur. They merely waited for some news.

News finally arrived in 1945, at the end of the war when a lucky survivor of the Death Railway came and told them what they had feared for a long time — that, Murugasu had indeed passed away while in Thailand. He had died in a strange country, surrounded by strange faces, knowing well that his family might be denied his last rites. On hearing the news, Rajambal merely carried on with life much as usual as the family wrestled with the fresh set of problems that end of war and the dissolution of the INA presented.

Only Bala knew in his heart that at 28, he had become the head of the family.

Return to Malaya

In 1928, when the GPO had been inaugurated at the Fullerton Building and the *Straits Times* had written of the "passing of old Singapore to the new", evidently, there had been an element of censure towards the "stately pile" because a mere two years ago the British authorities had decided to shift the postal headquarters to Kuala Lumpur.[19] In KL the headquarters were housed in the General Post Office, a beautiful specimen of Indo-Saracenic architecture designed by the British architect A B Hubback in 1896. True to his signature style, evident in many buildings spread over British Malaya, Hubback had incorporated wide arcaded verandas, a central leaf design pediment, fairy tale towers for winding staircases and a breezy arch walkway which connected it to the Sultan Abdul Samad Building or the Federal Secretariat down the road. But during the Japanese Occupation it all changed. The busy, pragmatic Nippon-zin spirit took over and with Singapore as the army headquarters and capital city, the Fullerton Building became home to the Japanese Military Administration. Closer to Fort Canning and with its open access to the sea, the building was a more functional choice for the army. The postal headquarters in turn were shifted to Kuala Lumpur, with the *Somuka* or Staff & General Affairs located not far away from the GPO at KL, its offices spread over two school buildings which again the British had built and the Japanese had taken over — the Victoria Institution and the Methodist Boys' School. Ironically both the schools, particularly the Victoria Institution located in Shaw Road (today's Jalan Hang Tuah), had been the crucible of British culture. Named to commemorate the coronation of Queen Victoria, it had been inspired by the Raffles Institution of Singapore, a place where the halls rang with the boys singing "*Victoria.... Victoria*", and where the distinctive E-shaped main block looked over expansive green playing fields where the Victoria Institution Cadet Corps, the oldest cadet corps of Malaya, trained.

By mid-1944 Bala was transferred along with the postal headquarters to Kuala Lumpur. Towards the beginning of the Japanese Occupation, he had been chosen by Katsuyoshi Akifuji, a senior officer of the *Somuka,* to work in the staff branch of the GPO in Singapore. It was on Bala's recommendation to Akifuji that his close friend Kandasamy too was selected to work in the *Kerika,* or Finance Department. Bala retains fond memories of his mentor and feels it was because of Katsuyoshi Akifuji's encouragement and guidance that he grew more confident in carrying out his duties. The two would remain in touch till much later after the war when Akifuji passed away.

With the move to KL, Bala found himself working again with the *Somuka,* which was set up first in the Victoria Institution and then moved to the Methodist Boys' School in Petaling Hill. They were not too far away from the GPO of KL which housed the Postal Headquarters as well as the Southern Division where he would work later. Yet again he was thrown together with his friend Kandasamy and the two bachelors were given living quarters at Galloway Road. A stone's throw from the Methodist Boys' School, they would walk to office from Galloway Road by crossing the railway track that ran at the end of the street.

Work was not difficult. Bala found both his Japanese and English writing skills came to good use and he worked on translation work, often setting English test papers for new employees as well as translating Japanese regulations into English for their use. The Postal Training Headquarters, earlier located in Battery Road, Singapore, had moved to a vacated Chinese school near the Methodist Boys' School and Bala found fruitful occupation here working on Japanese to English translation. He was also entrusted with distributing rationed cigarettes and rice and sugar to the postal staff and found he could even make a little money on the side by selling his own ration of cigarette packets on the black market. He discovered that despite naysayers, it was not difficult to work with the Japanese staff of the Postal Administration. They were often graduates from Japanese universities who had been mobilised for overseas military service and quickly understood local postal regulations and appreciated the problems of the staff. Though the officers were strict they never ill-treated the staff, in fact on the contrary, they often tried to obtain extra food supplies from the army for distribution to the local staff. Bala particularly has fond memories of one Saito Soichi San, an amenable officer who was a law graduate from Japan with a good command over English (though he scarcely if ever spoke in English), with whom he remained in touch long after the war was over. Bala would write letters to him in the *kanji* script and Saito San would reply also in Japanese but go out of his way to annotate the *kanji* in red to facilitate easier reading and understanding. Bala even travelled to Tokyo to meet him and his family living in Sendai, and Saito San in turn visited Bala in Singapore in 1999, by when the Japanese officer was 97 years old and in a wheelchair.

It was also while working in *Somuka* at the Methodist Boys' School that Bala became friends with a young Chinese gentleman called Lee Khee Wee. Khee Wee would visit Bala and Kandasamy in the Galloway Road government quarters along with his colleagues (Leong Seok Hong, Yap Yew Kau and Ooi Kwee Weng) and share the simple home-cooked meals they had prepared. As it turned out, this friendship too endured the test of time with Bala visiting Khee Wee in the UK when he worked as the Head of the Department of Oral Pathology at the Institute of Dental Surgery, London and Khee Wee in turn staying with Bala in his La Salle Street residence when he visited Singapore.

Despite financial difficulties and political uncertainties, during his stay in Petaling Hill, Bala found the pall of depression which had settled on him and his family in Singapore after Muragasu's departure finally lifting. Away from the ever-watchful eyes of Rajambal, he discovered life could offer simple pleasures — a simply cooked meal of rice and lentils with the assistance of 'Kanda' (Kandasamy) or a morning walk down the railway tracks could make him feel happy and at peace with himself.

Conclusion

By December 1941, life in Singapore had taken yet another turn. With the first Japanese air raids and stories of soldiers lying dead in trenches in the Keppel Barracks and the fierce battlefield of Blakang Mati (now Sentosa Island), Bala had known life would never be the same again. For a while his only role seemed to have been to seek safety when sirens went off and, like ghosts appearing out of the shadows, re-emerge from subterranean bomb shelters when the all-clear sounded. But then to everybody's surprise the British surrendered — the might of the empire was over, Singapore, the bastion of the east, was lost to the Japanese! As strange stories emerged of young English girls packing the last of their evening dresses for the summer balls of London, Bala never could decide what surprised him more — the fall of Britain or the victory of Japan.

Since then his life moved as if on fast forward. First the name of Singapore changed, then its language and then its time; the clock was set forward by one and a half hours to match the time in Tokyo.[20] Over a fortnight, the newspaper Bala was accustomed to reading changed not only its name from the *Straits Times* to the *Syonan Times,* but also did an about turn in content and spirit — there were cartoons lampooning Churchill and German capture of Anglo-American positions were suddenly events to be lauded. Familiar landmarks changed too — the shop windows of Whiteaway Laidlaw displayed Japanese soap rather than English smelling salt and at the Farrer Park there were bustling housewives tilling their plot of land for tapioca rather than sedate gentlemen out on an evening walk! Eurasians, who had prided themselves on being closest in line to the British, were labouring at construction sites, unceremoniously dressed in shorts and singlet, while Indians, as Japanese allies, had moved up a notch in the social ladder. Instead of looking to the west and singing *God Save the King*, Singapore was suddenly looking to the east and singing *Kimi Ga Yo*!

There are some important takeaways from the period of Japanese Occupation in the context of Bala's life. First and foremost, his experience of the Japanese was largely a positive one and perhaps more importantly, Bala is willing to go against the grain of popular opinion in voicing this. He shared a warm relationship with some of his Japanese officers and continued to stay in touch with them in the years to come. He would write to them in the *kanji* script and go out of his way to entertain his former *senseis* (teachers) when they visited Singapore and even paid them private visits in Japan and was warmly welcomed to their homes.

This is not only because as a part of the Indian community he received less hostile treatment in their hands than the Chinese or the Eurasians but because he genuinely appreciated some elements of their culture. His family went through its own share of misfortune during the Japanese rule. Bala recounts, this was a period when his central worry was one for food. The Japanese *Kumiai* would get more and more stringent in its regulation and food rations would steadily dwindle. He watched his *Amma* trying out all means — tapioca instead of rice, rice starch instead of milk, soya instead of meat. But even then they found it difficult to make ends meet.

Yet he was perceptive enough to look beyond the popular markers of Japanese culture — the tiffin dances at Great World, the star singers and vaudeville artists who were regularly called in to entertain soldiers at the Hibiya Public Hall or the many shophouses which were converted into geisha homes. Instead, he focussed on the true essence of the Nippon-zin — their *bushido* spirit of sacrificial nationalism, their respect for ancestral gods and elders and their ardour for enterprise. It nurtured in him a new sense of responsibility towards his family as well as loyalty towards country and culture while the industriousness remained with him in his career. There are only a few extant memoirs which speak of the Japanese rule with any fondness after the bloodbath and violence it unleashed, and Bala's remains one of them. Other than him there is Samad Ahmad, the Malaysian journalist for instance, who had a positive experience while working for the paper *Berita Malai* and the radio or the Roman-Catholic La Salle Brothers who after an initial period of incarceration were allowed a large measure of freedom by the Japanese.

Besides, the hidden romantic in Bala which had sought an outlet in reading Shakespeare under the British, during the Japanese Occupation turned for gratification to the fine aesthetics of Japanese culture — the Zen art of the tea ceremony and the perfect balance of the picturesque *kanji* script. By 1942 he would clear exams for the *kana* and *hiragana* courses and in the subsequent year enrol himself for the more advanced level available in learning Japanese — the exam for the *kanji* characters. He reminiscences, as he looked at the columns of neat strokes and radicals, he was often amazed by the beauty of what he had created. To him each character seemed to tell its own story. 山 — the character which represented a mountain which brought to his mind the snow-clad pinnacle of Mount Fuji; 火 — the character which represented fire and brought to mind the image of a cheerful log-fire; 雨 — the character which represented rain and evoked the sound of rain lashing against a closed window. Each stimulated his senses, conveying much more than the phonetic sound the Roman alphabets represented.

In fact for him, each character seemed to capture a bit of an ancient culture. Bala recalls the classes conducted by Kunitani, the principal of the *Kokugo Gakko* in Queen Street. He would explain to them, for instance the significance of the *kanji* character for the word 'world'. The Japanese word for 'world', *sekai, is a compound of two kanji characters:* 世 or *se* meaning generation and 界 *kai* meaning world. Bala would look at the first character carefully and catch himself wondering if 世 looked like a woman holding a child. And the second — 界 — didn't it look like a house? So the world was encapsulated in the figure of a mother and a home? His mind would go back to his own *Amma* at home, toiling day and night to keep them afloat, and a single word would teach him new lessons in not only respecting the older generations but also in serving his motherland to ensure the freedom of the future world.

It is also remarkable how different were his responses to the British and the Japanese rules. Toward both, he remains true to his nature and harbours little hostility. Yet, while the British remained distantly benign — denizens of a world which he could never hope to populate, only perhaps to serve, there was a new immediacy in his reaction to the Japanese. The obvious reason was of course because they were fellow Asians, closer to him in his mental reading of the racial ladder. But also, perhaps there was a certain involvement on his part which was actively nurtured by the Japanese. Unlike under the British, when he felt he was merely an instrument for fulfilling English instructions, a cog in the wheel of the great machinery of the Empire on which the sun never set, with the Japanese he was actually made to feel he could effectively contribute in building up a new world order. The whole Asia for the Asians concept, however contrived it might appear on hindsight, was important for second generation migrants like him in multi-racial Singapore who had never experienced any sense of personal participation under a largely indifferent British authority. Under the Japanese he experienced a sense of empowerment, however limited, and this excited him. It brought with itself new ideas and plans of shaping the migrant society of which he was a part.

So was he finally reconciled to the thought that he was to be an Indian living in Singapore? Had the transient status of the community finally changed? The answer would be no, but definitely a beginning had been made. The call of Subhas Chandra Bose to serve India and the cause of her freedom was a passionate one and could not be ignored. For the first time he felt an actual, tangible connection to his country, a connection that was far more forceful than the demands made by his parents to conform to Indian culture. Because Bose's call was backed by the nationalist cause it had a hard-to-ignore legitimacy. This was a time when patriotic music made forays into his consciousness. Bala was moved just as much by the INA's marching tune he had heard at the *Padang* — *Kadam kadam barae ja*, as he was by the popular Japanese patriotic song, *Aikoku Koshinkyoku* to which they marched at the *Kakugo Gakko*. Try as he might, Bala would not understand the lyrics of either of the songs. And yet, he wondered, why did they make his blood sing?

Like many from the diaspora he was captivated by the image of motherland that Bose held up for them: post-independent India, a country of fair participation and congenial brotherhood run on democratic, secular principles. The fantasy would of course be decimated by the partition of India and the ensuing communal riots, a situation closely reflected in the Hindu-Muslim riots of Singapore in 1946 when violence broke out in Kandang Kerbau, Kampong Java, Geylang Serai, etc.[21]

Like many others in his community, Bala would also vacillate between the pan-Indian call of Indian nationalism and the community-centric call of the Tamil associations. The root cause of this conflict was the ancient Aryan-Dravidian or the North Indian-South Indian divide which made Tamil residents of Singapore prickle at the thought of being labelled sectarian, while North Indians claimed they represented the interest of the entire Indian community. At the advent of the INA period he and his friends would decide to withdraw from the Tamils' Reform Association because they felt they needed to support the Indian National Congress and not the TRA, influenced as it was by the anti-Congress Justice Party and the Dravidian Self-Respect Movement of Periyar. However, by 1938, the two political strands (i.e., the Justice Party and the Self-Respect Movement) would merge in India and in 1944, E V Periyar Ramasamy would form the *Dravidar Kazagham* Party, a branch of which would be opened in Singapore and in which G Sarangapani would take the lead in reconstituting several Tamil organisations which had been marginalised during war.

There is also something rather remarkable about Bala's experience with the INA and with Subhas Chandra Bose. Here too his experience stands apart from popular understanding which normally pegs civilian reaction to the entire INA episode as one which was sudden and un-premeditated. But, as in Bala's case, it is impossible to read the emotional response as a single layer of unexpected passion. His mind and personality had already been shaped by his involvement with the IYL Movement and the food boycott which was staged by the senior Indian signallers at the Signal Company's camp. Along with this, the years of exposure to the Self-Respect Movement which culminated in his being a part of the TRA as well as the Nippon-zin spirit which he had imbibed, need to be taken into account for a full understanding of the situation. Thus, Bose's edicts fell on ground which had already been fertilised with thoughts of the unfairness of foreign rule. But at the same time, it is true that nothing prepared him for the way the 5th July speech at the *Padang* stirred him. Like many other young men and women of the Indian community, he felt strongly compelled to play a definitive role in the movement. Bose provided them with a viable role model which they had lacked earlier. As in the case of S R Nathan, former President of Singapore, in Bala's case too, the incubation period would be long and they would not plunge into the movement immediately but the heightened political awareness and sense of purpose would remain and influence their public life later.

There are a couple of more aspects in his experience which need to be highlighted. Firstly, he or his family did not face any kind of coercion from the INA — neither in terms of membership nor donations. There is a possibility that Murugasu heard of the Siam-Burma railway project at the IIL office, possibly at a time when the full horrors of the story had not unfolded, but finally he was forcibly taken away by the Japanese. As for the question whether the family's response to the INA was one triggered by patriotism or pragmatism, it would be safe to say, at least in Bala's case, that it was a combination of both. He was moved by the idea and genuinely frustrated that he could not join in the early frenzy to participate during July-August 1943. Possibly it was Murugasu's decision to keep his two daughters involved to a certain extent without committing the future of the family to the cause. After his disappearance in Thailand, by June 1944 the news of Anglo-American landings on the beaches of Normandy filtered in and Bala's own understanding of the war situation took over and broke his resolve. The timely transfer of the postal headquarters to KL offered him reprieve from his moral dilemma.

Finally, in his personal life, with the passing away of his father, life would never be the same again. Just as from now onwards he knew he would have to shoulder the responsibly of his family, it also meant that as the only male and the breadwinner, he had gone up a notch on the ladder of authority.

Notes

[1] S C Goho joined back the IIL only after Subhas Bose's advent in Singapore in July 1943.

[2] There are records which state that Commander J T Grist, Assistant Secretary to the Admiral in Sime Road ordered the burning of cypher books on the 12th of February.

[3] *Shonan Times,* 16 March 1942.

[4] *Kanji (J)* = the logographic Chinese characters adopted in Japanese script.

[5] *Kana (J)* = syllabic Japanese script; *Hiragana (J)* = cursive *kana* script

[6] The currency issued by the Japanese government during the Japanese Occupation of Singapore, Malaya, North Borneo, Sarawak and Brunei, so called because of the motif of banana trees on the $10 note.

[7] *Kumiai (J)* = guild to control supply of essential materials

[8] *Gunseikan-bu (J)* = Japanese military administration

[9] *Syonan Times,* 30 October 1942.

[10] *Bushido (J)* = warrior

[11] *Shonan Times,* 26 February 1942.

[12] For articles on making Nippon-Go the lingua franca of Malaya, see ibid, 9 March, 4 August, 25 October 1942.

[13] Details of postal employee training scheme from *The Postal History of the Occupation of Malaya and British Borneo: 1941–45,* Edward B Proud and Milo D Rowell. Postal History Publications, East Sussex, 1992.

¹⁴ P Ranga was a close friend under whose leadership Bala and his friends from the TRA joined the IYL in 1939. He had considerable knowledge of India and this had influenced Bala in the first place when he had eagerly joined the TRA. Bala, Ranga and two other friends had formed a close group which went by the sobriquet, the *Four Musketeers* and the *Singapore Free Press* of 28 June 1939 reports of a table tennis match between YMCA Juniors and TRC with the latter represented by K Sattappan, A G Sambandam (capt.), P Ranga, M Bala Subramanion etc. Later P Ranga would be repatriated to India because he was employed by the British Army's Administration Division and Bala would again meet him in 1967 during his visit to Tamil Nadu.

¹⁵ The *Syonan Times* of 5 August 1943 for instance which carried blaring headlines of Lord Linlithgrow, Viceroy of India who had been instructed by British Secretary of State to keep a close watch on Gandhi and Nehru.

¹⁶ The reports from *Syonan Sinbun*, 3rd July 1943.

¹⁷ In Singapore the tiger emblem used in Germany was dropped and the INA reverted back to flying the Congress tricolour.

¹⁸ Reportedly, the rates were higher than those publicised by the Labour Department, amounting to around a dollar a day and as news of the dismal working conditions spread, a compensation payment of $120 was announced and an added bonus of $50 to each labourer who returned on completion of his contract.

¹⁹ *Straits Times,* 27 June 1928.

²⁰ The reference here is to the fact that under the Japanese, two timings were maintained, one was the local time and one was the Tokyo time which was one and a half hours ahead of the local time to match the time in Japan. While under the British, Singapore and Malaya was divided into the Straits Settlements, the Federated Malay States and the Unfederated Malay States, each with its own administrative priorities and preoccupations, under the Japanese, Singapore would be renamed *Syonan-to* and Malaya *Malai*, the latter divided into eight provinces each with a Japanese as governor and a sultan as the vice-chairman of the Council.

²¹ *The Indian Minority and Political Change in Malaya, 1945–1957*, Ampalavanar R. Oxford University Press, Kuala Lumpur, 1981. pp. 28–29.

1942–1945. Staff of the General Post Office during the Japanese Occupation, in front of the Fullerton Building. On the pillars is written in *kanji* script, "Syonan-to Central Post Office".

1943. Graduation of students from Malaya, at *Kokugo Gakko* on Queen Street, Syonan-to.
Sitting. Fourth from left: Kunitani Sensei.
Middle row, standing. Fifth from left: Bala.

1943. A Japanese prize winning shield awarded to Bala by *Kokugo Gakko* on Queen Street, Syonan-to, for being the top student in the *Kotoka* (Advanced course in Japanese).

1969. Bala and wife Sumitra with Akifuji and his daughter in Hiroshima, Japan.

1999. Saito Soichi seated in a wheelchair and accompanied by two daughters Hiromi and Mayumi at the Singapore Botanical Gardens, during his first post-war visit to Singapore.

2005. Bala in Sendai, Japan, with Prof Miyawaki Hiroyuki, a friend of Saito, who had visited Singapore to do research on the educational system during the Japanese Occupation.

2007. Bala with Lee Khee Wee, London, UK.

2010. In Kerala with K M S Hamid, Bala's close friend from *Kokugo Gakko* days and thereafter.

CHAPTER 4

Gave Him a Cause

Post Second World War: 1945–1956

"There was in him a cool Confucian smile.
Some suitable history would have been
A place in the Family Bank,
Consolidated by a careful match,
A notable gain in family wealth,
…An ordinary life, ordinary longevity.
Of these things his father sadly dreams.
He was not made for politics.
…The new people took him in to cells, discussions;
Exciting oratory. Gave him a cause."

The Exile, Singapore
— *Edwin Thumboo*

End of Japanese Rule

The Japanese Occupation found Bala dividing his time between Singapore and Kuala Lumpur. Previously under the British the Postal HQ had been located in KL with the financial as well as administrative functions centralised there while the Fullerton Building of Singapore housed the day-to-day postal service for the city and the world beyond. But under the Japanese, initially, a considerable number of senior staff and officers were reengaged and relocated from KL to Singapore and the Fullerton became the official headquarters with functions divided into three broad categories — *Kerika* (Finance), *Somuka* (Staff & General Affairs) and *Gyomuka* (Postal Services). This arrangement, however, again changed in 1944 when the headquarters were shifted back to KL (housed first in the Victoria Institution and then the Methodist Boys' School, not too far from the GPO near the present day Federal Secretariat Building), possibly keeping in view the proximity of the Fullerton Building to the open sea which left it vulnerable to external attack. Thus from 1944 onwards, Bala, a part of the *Somuka* or the Staff & General Affairs Department, found himself in KL, working in the postal offices established first in the Victoria Institution and then the Methodist Boys' School in Petaling Hill. In 1946 the Straits Settlements were dissolved, Penang and Malacca were absorbed into the Malayan Union while Singapore became a separate Crown Colony. But despite this, the postal services like telecommunications continued to be administered on a pan-Malayan basis and in fact in August 1949, Singapore and the Federation of Malaya signed an agreement known as the Postal Union of Malaya Agreement whereby both territories formed a single postal area.

Cut away for the first time from the apron strings of his mother, Bala found life to be quite pleasant. He got along well with his Japanese bosses and the presence of his friend Kandasamy made life all the more agreeable. Japanese propaganda in newspapers and on the radio raged strong and they had little inkling that the fate of the Axis Powers was gradually turning or that the Western Allies had completed preparations for the final drive into Germany's heart. Thus, 19th February 1945, when the US Air Force bombed KL for the first time, it came as a shock to both him and Kanda. The two of them along with other postal staff members crouched on the high grounds of the Victoria Institution to watch the spectacular sight of the B29 heavy bombers dropping huge loads of explosives on the Sentul Railway District. The British Forces had not given any prior warning of the attack and the residents of KL simply looked on as the explosives fell. The target was the Central Workshops of the Federated Malay States Railway or what had been renamed the Marai Tetsudo by the Japanese. Bala looked on as most of the workshops where the finest British locomotives and coaches had once been assembled, as well as the surrounding staff colonies which housed a largely Indian population of railway workers, were reduced to rubble. He had known Sentul chiefly as a railway workers' colony and a place where annually large groups of Murugan devotees congregated to visit the Batu Caves during Thaipusam. Now as he watched the destruction wrought by the bombing, he felt a sense of apprehension but he also knew it to be a clear indication that the British-American forces were on the move to recover their lost territories in the East; that soon their lives would be changing again and that soon his mettle would be put to test again.

It was soon after this that he heard of his mother not keeping good health and applied to his Japanese head of department for a transfer back to Singapore. The Japanese responded with sympathy and thus, by July 1945 Bala was back with his family in Singapore and it was here that he heard of the bombing of Hiroshima and Nagasaki and watched as the victorious British Military rolled back into power. The Japanese rule was decisively at an end.

An Unfamiliar Step in Familiar Singapore

Bala watched the return of the British with new, 28-year-old eyes and realised just how difficult everyday survival had become. As the one responsible for putting food on the family table, the grimness of the post-war situation hit him every day. A postal clerk writing for the *Telepost*, the official publication of the Singapore Union of Postal and Telecommunications Workers which would be started by Bala and his colleagues soon, would describe the situation as one which was "replete with dangers for any bachelor", for no young man who entered the postal services could dare to get married. Any young man joining government services knew that he, for more than 25 years from the time he joined as a clerk would have to labour slowly up the government spiral staircase to the top where the salary was S$250 per month. And he asked, could the British government blame them if the Japanese Occupation and the subsequent period of uncertainty had led to a certain amount of decline in moral standards?[1] Yet another young clerk writing for the same journal would comment on his family being reduced to starvation levels. While earlier a clerk belonged to the respectable middle-class, now they were forced to work as menials, often peddling trishaws after office hours to make those extra few cents; their dress was shabby, they were undernourished, living in rented rooms in overcrowded tenements. And consequently, the public treated them with little respect, more like servants than government employees.[2]

Lee Kuan Yew, who by 1946 would start preparing to leave Singapore to study law in Cambridge with a suitcase full of warm clothes bought from the Sungei Road flea market, writes of the period immediately after the return of the British as a period of liberation which did not bring what everybody wanted: punishment of the wicked and reward for the virtuous. A sense of resentment developed, particularly among the Chinese community who had borne the brunt of Japanese atrocities, as the British, handicapped by lack of evidence and documentation, appeared to be too lenient towards Japanese war criminals. The bitterness would exacerbate as the British failed to offer the MPAJA (Malayan People's Anti-Japanese Army), which consisted primarily of Chinese volunteers, the status and freedom it felt it rightfully deserved.

On the other hand, S R Nathan, the future President of Singapore, who at that time was staying in Johor, working as a temporary clerk with the Public Works Department of the Johor state government, writes of the hostility bred among Malay nationalists towards the British. The Malay Nationalist Party, led by Dr Hamzah for instance, considered itself nationalist and wanted Malaya to be an independent republic of the kind that Indonesia then aspired to be and thus considered the pro-Sultan, relatively pro-British Malay organisations like the UMNO to be feudalistic. And lastly, there was the Indian community, which though a minority, had taken firm steps towards leadership and nationalism under Subhas Chandra Bose during the Japanese Occupation and would soon have their confidence further bolstered by their country achieving independence. Thus, though initially the returning British were welcomed after the oppressive Japanese rule, it did not take too long for relationships to sour and it was soon evident that there was no way the British could ignore the intervening years of ethnic nationalism.

If ethnic tensions and a dismal economic scenario were not enough, the situation was greatly exacerbated by the presence of the communists. In fact, as the labour leader and founder of Singapore's National Trades Union Congress C V Devan Nair points out, between the years 1945–1948 most of the political unrest of the time rode on the backs of communists.[3] The MCP (Malayan Communist Party) had been founded in 1930 but more important was its rise to prominence from towards the end of Japanese rule to the interregnum between the fall of the Japanese on 15th August 1945 and the restoration of British civilian rule in April 1946. Large numbers of MCP affiliates had formed the core of the MPAJA and by the end of war, the MPAJA guerrilla emerged as popular heroes. They had been trained and armed by the Allied South East Asian Command and had aided the British in waging guerrilla warfare against the Japanese. Consequently, under the British Military Administration, the communists emerged from underground as the MCP was allowed to operate openly for the first time and the MPAJA was lavished with praise for its role in building resistance and sabotaging Japanese missions. After September 1945, though the MPAJA came under British pressure and reluctantly disbanded, with formal ceremonies held where weapons were surrendered, the communists remained sceptical of British emasculation and retained a proportion of their weapons which they intended to use in their red revolution. This would mean that in the future too the communist-backed worker unions would continue to be associated with a certain militant culture and irresponsible bravado, while communist trade union leaders would be hailed as folk heroes, known for their highly charged, euphuistic speeches.

It was against this background that Bala, by September 1945, realised that the Engineering Division of the P & T Department where he had earlier worked under the British, had been reconstituted as the Singapore Telecommunication Department and formed a separate organisation. But with the majority of his friends still in postal service, he decided to return to work as a part of the Mails Branch in the Singapore GPO. This was despite the training he had received under the Engineering Division and the considerable level of competence he had been able to master in establishing telecommunication infrastructure.

On return the first thing that struck him was the difficulties under which he and his colleagues had to labour. By December 1945 the rice ration per week had been reduced to 3 *katis* (600 grams) and families were on the verge of starvation while British soldiers of the BMA, knowing that they would be stationed in Malaya only briefly till demobilisation orders arrived, made the most of it. As Turnbull says, the black market enterprise which had earlier attracted the worst sort of Japanese now brought in the most corrupt Westerner. Bala, concerned about the situation, started volunteering after office hours at the post office club and soon found he had been appointed secretary of the Staff Welfare Committee.

The post-war period was essentially a time when trade unionism began in Singapore. Though Chinese guilds or *hongs* had been operating in Singapore for over a century, they functioned almost like the craft guilds of the middle-ages and were useful in settling disputes and determining terms of employment for traditions trades and crafts. In fact over the years some of these guilds had been associated with Chinese secret societies and had little or no role in organising unskilled industrial labour. It was in October 1945 that the Singapore General Labour Union was launched by the MCP at the Happy World Amusement Park. Within the next few weeks the GLU was able to establish its control over the unions across the causeway as well and by mid-1947, its affiliates included 72 of the total 126 unions across Malaya with a membership of over 56,000. Over the course of these years the GLU would be first known as the Pan-Malayan General Labour Union. But from August 1946 onwards the Singapore GLU would be forced under British regulation to separate from the Malayan GLU and the SGLU would be renamed the SFTU (Singapore Federation of Trade Unions). Yet what would not change was the MCP's hold over the union, its powerful mass base and by implication its control over some of the vital sectors of the economy including transport, communication and essential services, while the SFTU became the main source of funds for the MCP.

In 1947 alone a total of 45 strikes occurred, resulting in a loss of 492,708 man days. Understandably, the British were concerned and keen on organising non-communist unions which would successfully curb the influence of the SFTU. With this in mind, in 1946, S P Garrett, a British trade unionist was appointed as an Assistant Trade Union Adviser, solely responsible for organising non-communist trade unions and reforming the SFTU. Though Garrett proved to be quite unpopular among both employers and employees, the British also around this time decided to implement more effectively the provisions of the Trade Union Ordinance of 1940 and consequently a number of unions, including the SFTU, were registered. This was in part a response to the increasing radical slant apparent in post-war Asia as it was a reflection of the political scenario in Britain where the Labour Party had returned to power with a landslide victory in 1945. Influenced as it was by the Fabian Society, the Labour Party preached the principle of "municipal socialism". They sought to offset the effects of unemployment and poverty as best they could while staying within existing structures and without the direct action urged by the fledgling communist party of Great Britain.

British attempts to encourage the formation of non-communist trade unions in Singapore had its greatest impact among the English-educated employees of the public service. And it is here that one of Bala's most critical early contributions lie. In the course of his volunteer work with the Staff Welfare Committee, he came in contact with senior staff members and they formed a small informal group to discuss ways of improving the service conditions of the staff. When in 1946 the Trade Union Ordinance became effective, the group decided to form a union in the long term interest of the workers. In the meantime, a copy of the British Post Officer Workers' Union constitution came into their hands and they used it as a model to frame the rules of the proposed union. In their discussions they were able to draw in the staff of the Telecommunication Department as well, so that a united front of the P & T employees could be presented. Trade Union Adviser S P Garrett as well as Commissioner for Labour Robert Porter Bingham helped in finalising the union rules and on 29th December 1946, the Singapore Union of Postal and Telecommunication Workers was founded. It would be formally registered on 31st March 1947, the first government union to be established for all workers in the two departments, including the uniformed and non-uniformed staff of all ranks, and Bala would be elected the first General Secretary of the Union.[4] The Executive Committee was a multi-racial one consisting of names (besides Bala) like P L Anthony, Paul Ng Fook Chin, Tay Tong Seng, Wong Peng Swee, Osman bin Faraj, Choo Koh Eng, Ismail bin Bachik, Tai Chong Cheong, Jafar bin Idris, Kadir bin Abdul Rahman, P Govindaswamy, Wee Kim Leong and Bala's long-time friend, G Kandasamy.[5] The profile of these men was quite similar — young, angry about the society around them, having undergone acute hardships in their time. None of them had any political affiliation and yet the group was politicised by dint of their exposure to the ethnic nationalist struggle during the war years — the Chinese were influenced by Sun Yat Sen and the Chinese Revolution, the Indians by the Indian independence struggle and the INA and the Malays by Sukarno and Hatta of Indonesia.

However, the unity between the uniformed and the junior clerks and the white-collared staff proved to be short-lived. The white-collared staff had been quite sceptical about the idea of a single union right from the beginning because their number was in minority and they felt they might be dominated by the other union members. The SFTU, uncomfortable at the thought of a union being formed outside their folds, played on this sense of distrust and within four months' time, by July 1947, the uniformed staff broke away and formed the Uniformed Postal Staff Workers' Union, associated with the SFTU, with an initial membership of 300, while the Union of Postal and Telecommunication Workers remained with a depleted membership of 458. Though Bala and his team members were disappointed at this, they continued to maintain a cordial relationship with the uniformed staff who were themselves quite disillusioned with their parent body, the SFTU. Members like Ismail bin Bachik, Jafar bin Idris and P Govindaswamy, who had been among the founding members of the Union of Postal and Telecommunication Workers, could not secure leadership positions for themselves in the new set up since they were opposed to the communists who dominated the SFTU. Consequently in 1947, when the Postal Services Joint Committee was established as a joint commission between employers and employees on the lines of the British Whitley Council, Bala was able to convince the members of the Uniformed Workers' Union to join in, which greatly enhanced the strength of the staff. Bala would become the Secretary representing the employees, and the alliance between the uniformed and non-uniformed staff would work well this time, based as it was on a clear understanding that neither would take any decision without prior consultation with the other. From this period till around 1959 when the Amalgamated Union of Public Employees was formed, though the two unions maintained their separate identities, the cohesion between them remained strong.

One of the most critical issues that the P & T Workers' Union handled was the arrear payment of salaries to government servants for the Japanese Occupation period, i.e., 1942–45. The British administration had decided to pay in full all salaries due to the European civil servants but only three months' salary or pension, subject to a maximum of $250, to its Asian employees. Such blatant discrimination obviously created considerable unhappiness among Asian workers and as S R Nathan points out, the back-pay issue became a "protracted and complex wrangle" between the British and the trade unions.[6] In early 1947, several unions, including the Singapore Postal and Telecommunication Workers' Union, the Singapore Teachers' Union, the Hospital Assistants and Dressers' Association, and the Police Inspector's Association joined in to form a collaborative body called the Singapore Civil Servants' Back Pay Council under the leadership of Dr A A Sandhosham. The Council had a meeting at the Civil Service Club and organised a mass public meeting on 24th March 1947 in the large football field in which Bala too participated and passed a resolution demanding full arrear payment of salary. Though the Council's demands were not successful, the issue remained in the public eye over a prolonged period with the Singapore newspapers reporting all subsequent meetings, including a joint mass rally planned in May 1947 between the Singapore Civil Servants' Back Pay Council and the Malayan Union Junior Civil Service Association. Even as late as September 1950, the *Straits Times* reports of the issue being raised by the Council Chairman A A Sandhosham at the annual meeting of the Singapore Civil Service Association.

When asked about the lack of success of the Back Pay Council, the postal union's first big endeavour, Bala says it left him disappointed but undeterred. He realised he was at the starting point of an exciting new journey in which setbacks would be many. In fact during the ensuing years, there have been several critics of unions such as the Singapore Postal and Telecommunication Workers' Union, nurtured as they were by the British with a clear intent of undermining the communists. C V Devan Nair himself, member of the People's Action Party and the third President of Singapore, writes of them rather disparagingly, "And [the British] introduced a trade union ordinance of sorts; and of course, very foolishly, they thought that they could compete with trade union groups inspired and organised by the Malayan communists…Those were days immediately after the World War when you had chaps like Jack Brazier and Simpson telling everybody how we ought to become replicas of the British trade union movement."[7] While such a view might have some following, it is equally true that a union such as the Postal and Telecommunication Workers' Union or the other trade unions which were registered under the British Ordinance between 1946 and 1950 played their own pioneering role. They were critical because they helped establish a rational culture of employer-employee negotiation by the use of legal means which would later be followed by the Amalgamated Union of Public Employees (AUPE) and continued even more emphatically by the National Trades Union Congress (NTUC) when it was formed in 1961. Such a culture would prove to be an important alternative during the turbulent 1950s when trade unionism degenerated into communist-instigated militancy, a period which Lee Kuan Yew describes as a time when Singapore fell in the grip of a "strike fest".

Forging On: Continuing Union Activities

In an attempt to take the Postal and Telecommunication Workers' Union a step ahead, Bala and his colleagues on the Executive Committee started establishing links with similar postal unions of Malaya. They planned to organise a Pan-Malayan Postal Union to further strengthen the workers' cause. This was possibly after the lukewarm response the Back Pay Council received from the government. The Uniformed Postal

Staff Workers' Union's call to strike had also met with relative failure with the government threatening the striking workers with dismissal with a month's notice. On 7th October 1947 the *Straits Times* reports that the British government had refused to be cowed by threats of a strike and when the Uniformed Postal Staff Workers' Union had submitted an ultimatum they had merely replied that a dismissal of a worker would entail forfeiture of all gratuities, retiring allowances, leave and other privileges and instead said that in anticipation of the strike the Singapore postal authorities would stop receiving parcels and registered letters since in case the strike did occur they would not be able to guarantee the safekeeping of such items. The objective of the strike had been to receive a 40% increase in wages and a $30 cost of living allowance, but all five representative unions including those of North Malaya, Perak, Selangor, Negeri Sembilan and Singapore had received a firm denial.

Given the circumstances, it is possible that Bala and his colleagues felt that the Postal and Telecommunication Workers' Union needed to be further strengthened, if they were to achieve anything at all without displaying the disruptive style advocated by the communists. In an attempt to organise a Pan-Malayan Postal Union, the post-office club secretaries from the various states were contacted and a conference of state representatives was organised in Kuala Lumpur with Bala as a member of the Singapore delegation. However though the discussions were lively, their attempt to gain strength in numbers did not meet with much success and Bala found a lack of collective will to pursue the project earnestly from the other side of the causeway. It needs to be remembered that by March 1946 the BMA had been replaced by a Malayan Union and consisted of the Federated Malay States, the Non-Federated Malay States and the former Straits Settlements with the exception of Singapore which was separately administered as a Crown Colony. The Malayan Union was marked by a rise in Malay nationalism which had as its corollary a certain sense of uncertainty towards Chinese-predominant Singapore.

Despite the not very cordial response to the idea of a Pan-Malayan Postal Union, Bala and his colleagues did not want to give up on the idea of a collaborative relationship and so instead launched a monthly postal review called *The Telepost* which would be circulated to Malacca and Penang union representatives as well, and so help maintain a close relationship. Bala was on the editorial board of the magazine and *The Telepost*, while it remained in circulation, proved to be quite a useful record of the times. Thus in August 1947 there appeared an article by the Registrar of Unions, P J Steele, who praised the Postal and Telecommunication Workers' Union for desisting from "gangsterism" and following legitimate means — a clear indication of the work ethic the British wanted to espouse. Again, in September 1948, there is an article which voices worker disappointment at the revised salary scales recommended for P&T staff by the Public Services Salaries Commission. The article states that the Commission had recommended a smaller percentage rise for the lower income groups and a larger one for the higher income groups and concludes rather bitterly that, "It is most distressing to note that while the Labour Government of Great Britain is trying to avoid social cleavages through inequality of incomes, the Colonial Government has thought it fit to accept proposals which would bring about even greater class differences among its people that those which existed before." Again a clear indication of the union's attempt to answer the government back with its own coin and build an irrefutable argument.

In fact, this attempt at educating the union members so that they could be on the same plane as the European employers and could engage in a meaningful discussion without it degenerating into either a one-sided conversation or a violent exchange would remain a major preoccupation for Bala and his colleagues. And with the aim of the educational advancement of its members, the Singapore P & T Union would become an affiliate to the Labour College of Scotland. The Labour College with its evening classes spread over Glasgow, Aberdeen, Dundee and Edinburgh, had been modelled on the Central Labour

College of London, the latter being a higher education institute supported by the Railwaymen's Union and the miners of South Wales which fitted in well in the Labour Party's larger plan of bringing education closer to industry. The Labour College of Scotland had a mission of providing subsidised education to disadvantaged or excluded adults who in turn could use it as a tool for progressive social change. Various correspondence courses for adults on subjects like political history, sociology, the history of the labour movement and psychology were on offer. Bala enrolled himself for a correspondence course on trade union management. It was an economically viable option and Bala's assignments would come back after being duly corrected in Scotland via sea mail. Most workers of Commonwealth countries had undergone testing times during the war and so it was easy to find a common cause.

The urge to widen the horizons remained with the Singapore P & T Workers' Union and as a next step the Executive Committee tried to establish contact with the other postal unions of Commonwealth countries. One of the first with which they were successful in establishing contact was the Postal Workers' Union of the UK which was an amalgamation of telephone, telegraph and postal workers.[8] Unfortunately, an affiliation with the UK union could not be sought because of its constitution which forbade such international alliances. But a greater breakthrough came in the form of an affiliation with the International Postal Workers' Union, headquartered in Bern, Switzerland which after the formation of the United Nations, became a specialised agency of the UN, meant for coordinating employment-related policies for postal workers across member countries. This was possibly the first time that a trade union from Singapore had received an affiliation to an international workers' organisation.

This was also a time when Bala found himself influenced by the principles preached by the Malayan Democratic Union (MDU). In the course of his activities with the Back Pay Council he had come in contact with P V Sharma, a Brahmin school teacher who championed the rights of Asian educators in relation to their expatriate counterparts and was the Secretary of the Singapore Teachers' Union. It was he who persuaded Bala to join the MDU. Founded on 21st December 1945, the MDU was the first local political party to be formed in Singapore after the war. It was a multiracial party formed by English educated young men who espoused the principle that the Malayan Union should be formed but insisted that Singapore should be a part of it. When it started, unlike the left-wing radicals, the MDU's was a lone moderate voice advocating social and educational reform, multi-lingualism and democratic trade unions. Bala found himself, along with Kandasamy and other colleagues from the Singapore P & T Workers' Union, regularly attending the lectures conducted by the MDU on political ideologies like Marxism and socialism. The classes would normally be held in the evening, after office hours at the MDU office at Liberty Cabaret (later the site was taken over by the Cathay Organisation's flagship cinema, the Odeon) at the junction of North Bridge Road and Cashin Street and it is here that Bala would be introduced to the idea of democratic socialism, a political philosophy widely espoused in Singapore during later years. But though Bala fully subscribed to the MDU manifesto, he also needed to be cautious since as a unionist he was prohibited from political involvement and needed to restrict himself solely to worker welfare activities.

In mid-1947 the debate on the possibility of introducing income tax in Singapore and the Malayan Union was initiated. It was a time when the British government, sorely pressed for revenues, had appointed R B Heasman as tax advisor to the two governments of Singapore and Malaya and was in the process of making recommendations and framing legislations. By August 1947 Heaseman would submit his report recommending the imposition of income tax on a pan-Malayan basis at a uniform flat rate of 20% for companies and personal taxation beginning at income levels of $250 per month.[9] As expected, there would be stiff opposition from commercial and business groups with the debate raging on for the next few years. The Indian businessman

R Jumabhoy would go on record to speak against it in the Singapore Legislative Council in September 1952, mentioning that during a time of economic slump, the imposition of income tax would mean a further drying up of precious foreign capital and wondering how Hong Kong could afford to have a lower tax structure than Singapore, given both were free ports and depended on entrepôt trade.

The MDU was one of the only associations which spoke in favour of the introduction of income tax and recommended instead that such income as the government made from the tax should be ploughed back to finance social improvement projects. The Singapore P & T Workers' Union which had judiciously been kept away from any kind of politicisation or influence of the communist-dominated SFTU, would in this case side with the MDU and support the introduction of income tax but insist that the proceeds be used by the government in welfare measures.

Thus during the years immediately following the war, Bala remained actively involved in not only his job but also union related work. It was a time when his life was taking a new turn, propelling him into leadership positions which he had never envisaged for himself. There was little time to devote to his family or to think of marriage. Unknown to him, Providence was smiling a kindly smile and yet further opportunities would come his way which would take him farther afield from home and hearth.

Even Wider Horizons Beckon: UK

The separation of Singapore as a Crown Colony, though not supported by the majority of its residents because of the impending threat of separation from Malaya, also had positive ramifications. It meant the British paid more attention to Singapore with the intent of building up local loyalties. As a part of such interventions the British government made known its intention of training members of the local populace for higher echelons of the Singapore Civil Service. And to his surprise, in December 1948 Bala came to know that he had been one of the first to be chosen to go to the UK under the Singapore Government Departmental Scholarship Scheme. It would be a two-year course in advanced postal training and Bala gladly accepted the appointment. This meant that the initial years of the Malayan Emergency would pass him by. Emergency would be declared in the Federation on 16th June 1948 and within a week, extend to Singapore.

It was time to pass on the baton of the Singapore P & T Workers' Union to a colleague and Bala ruminated on this with some sadness. He had helped establish the union and the last few years had been spent in ceaseless attempts to place it on a strong foundation. It was particularly sad because it was only of late that the union had seen the first signs of success with not only its international affiliation but also with the Singapore Government finally accepting to review the time-scale salary pay plan and the increase of the initial salary of women workers to match that of the men. The prickly issue of the cost-of living allowance had been broached by the union as early as in January 1947 and then there had been the matter of the arrear payment of wages as well as protests over low initial pay and an annual increment of $5. Initially the union's recommendations had been submitted to the Salaries Commission. But the Commission's decisions had not been acceptable to the union and it was only in 1948 that the proposal had gone up for review to the joint Singapore and Federation of Malaya Committee and the union was hopeful of better justice.[10]

After some deliberation the stewardship of the postal union as well as of the Postal Services Joint Council was handed over to G Kandasamy, Bala's old friend from the Japanese Occupation period and one who had worked closely with him as the Assistant Secretary of the P & T Workers' Union. In the subsequent years Kandasamy would of course play a vital and high-profile role as a trade unionist, coming in close contact with the future President of Singapore, S R Nathan, when in the 1950s the latter was Welfare Officer of the Seamen's Union. In 1952, Kandasamy would invite the Cambridge-returned young lawyer

Lee Kuan Yew as the P & T Union's legal advisor and the ensuing legal case between the government and the union would receive substantial coverage in local newspapers and finally succeed in obtaining better pay and conditions for the postal workers. In 1957 Kandasamy would be elected Secretary General of the Singapore Trade Union Congress, and once the STUC was dissolved, would form the National Trades Union Congress while Bala would charter his own path of success in the postal services and in his work with the Indian community.

The *Straits Times* of 23rd December 1948 writes of Bala being chosen as the first member of the Singapore Postal Services Department to go to England. He had been selected along with Douglas Clunies-Ross, yet another postal employee who was also one of the best all-rounder sportsmen of the island and a descendent of the famous Clunies-Ross dynasty, the self-proclaimed kings and proprietors of the Cocos and Keeling Islands. They set sail on 4th January on board the Dutch liner, the *Willem Ruys*, the same ship which Lee Kuan Yew and his newly wedded wife would take for their return journey from Cambridge in 1950. Bala found the meals on the ship to be sumptuous (Lee Kuan Yew too comments on the excellent Indonesian and Dutch food) and though he partook of the lavish meals with some satisfaction, as a trade unionist he could not help but think of the sparse meals most working class families like his could afford back in Singapore. He also found that at times he faulted in his table manners and in the use of the right cutlery and was glad for the presence of Clunies-Ross at his elbow to correct him.

The *Willem Ruys* was a new cruise ship, having been built in 1947 by the Royal Rotterdam Lloyd Company, and so was fitted out with modern features. Not only were there a library and a smoking room for the first class passengers but also a cinema lounge and a winter garden and outdoor swimming pools accessible to everybody. But while Bala was impressed by such amenities, to his surprise and perhaps even dismay, even in the high seas he found no possibility of the loosening up of racial hierarchical rules which had so overtaken his life since birth. As expected, Europeans travelled in the air conditioned first class cabins and occupied the first class deck while he along with the other Asians on board enjoyed each other's company in the tourist class. In fact, the Bengali doctor Aroon Kumar Sinha, who was to be a prominent obstetrician and gynaecologist at the Kandang Kerbau Maternity Hospital of Singapore in the future, was en route to London as well. Sinha, travelling to the UK for his post-graduate degree, was travelling first class and yet felt more at ease to come down to the tourist class deck to keep company with them. More disturbing for Bala were the numerous Indonesian stewards in native dress. He noticed their abject subservience to the Dutch officers and could not help but feel uncomfortable.

But otherwise it turned out to be a very pleasurable journey and Bala felt little seasickness even on the Bay of Biscay, notorious for bringing down the most sea-worthy sailors. The ship docked first at Colombo and then having passed through the Suez Channel, reached the English port of Southampton on 23rd January 1949, a record journey of 19 days as compared to the customary 21 days.

From the port he took a train to London and found himself in an unfamiliar city, caught up in the depth of winter. Bala could not recall ever feeling so cold.

Post-War Europe and a Malayan Identity

Bala and Clunies-Ross reached the British Council Hostel in Queen's Gate Garden, London. He was in one of the oldest cities of the world, a city which sat astride the River Thames and had a history that went back a millennium and more. Signs of the war were everywhere. Obviously, the blitz had hit the city really hard and residents vividly remembered that morning when the German Luftwaffe filled the skies. Yet Bala realised there was a certain resilience in the way Londoners seemed to be handling the aftermath of war. He noticed construction happening everywhere — out of the rubble were rising here a hospital, there a school and what looked like an large office building. And as he spent more time in the city he realised that just as Londoners spoke about the destruction wrought by war, they also liked to talk about the discoveries unearthed by the bombings — a Roman wall at Cripplegate, a Gothic doorway at St Vedast's — symbols of a proud past which buoyed up and provided courage for the present.

They stayed for a week at the hostel and during this time he became more familiar with English ways. He was taken to Hyde Park and marvelled at the freedom of expression the citizens enjoyed, the way the English greeted strangers on the road and the way they queued up in an orderly manner despite obvious shortages and food rationing. Bala remembers his worst struggle was with the cold. The building had no central heating and the electric heaters in the bedrooms seemed to gobble up an inordinate number of coins. Finally Bala took to warming his pillows on the heating coils before he went to bed. The hostel housed a cosmopolitan crowd — students who had come from far off countries of the Commonwealth — Africa and the West Indies — and Bala enjoyed getting to know about their country and culture. This was also true for the streets of London. Contrary to what he had expected, there was a fair sprinkling of other nationalities on the streets, including Asians. He was told they were immigrants from the far-flung colonies of the Empire and the trend had become more prominent of late in anticipation of post-war decolonisation by the British.

From London they took a train to Shrewsbury and it was here that Bala's training began in earnest. He soon learnt that they would be initially posted in Shropshire and then move to Southampton, Cardiff and finally to the London GPO which was incidentally the financial, administrative and international headquarters of the British Post Office. They were posted for about a year at Shrewsbury. Initially everything seemed unfamiliar including the name of the town which was spelt Shrewsbury and yet pronounced *shrosebury*. But gradually the market town, caught in a loop of the River Savern, the town of Charles Darwin and Wilfred Owen with its timber framed houses and steep, narrow streets grew on him. He learnt that the room they rented with bed and breakfast and managed by two elderly sisters was to be referred to as 'digs'. And that he could take a bath only once a week because of coal rationing and that he needed to pay an extra fee for the privilege of having an electric heater operating in his bedroom during winter. It was in Shrewsbury that he attended courses connected with all facets of a postman's work including mail sorting, counter service and delivery. At the end of each such training course he travelled to the Wellington Post Office, which was a short train trip away, for practical work exposure and each such visit turned out to be an enriching experience. At times he would accompany a postman on his cycle or at times don a mechanic's overalls to work with the vehicle supervisor in the maintenance of postal vans. He remembers at times he had to walk for three hours at a stretch on his postal beats in the English countryside. This would be early in the morning because the day's mail needed to reach residents before they left for work and though physically exacting, Bala would be completely overwhelmed by the sheer beauty of the rolling landscape. At the Wellington Head Post Office while working at the counter he experienced what appeared to be a cordial atmosphere. The English customers were curious seeing a dark young man serving at the counter and wanted to know which country he came from. They had not heard of Singapore or in which part of the colony it was located, some merely associated it with China. Yet they were polite and smiled and expressed surprise at the dexterity with which Bala could deal with their currency — the pounds, crowns and shillings. However, later the Head Postmaster confided in him that some of his friends had expressed some disquiet about the fact that despite local unemployment problems the post office had thought it fit to employ a foreigner at the counter, a disquiet that was quickly doused by the Head Postmaster confirming that Bala was a temporary trainee.

Shrewsbury is a town which is known for its pubs and on weekends Bala would often accompany his friends when they went pub-crawling. Although at first his Hindu upbringing compelled him to abstain, he soon learned to relax and join his friends in the merriment of the evenings, greatly enjoying the discussions and the loud laughter. He would often visit the cinemas as well because he found it to be an easy way to stretch out his weekly allowance of about six pounds. The cinemas were cheap and cosy retreats from the winter chill and films were run throughout the day without breaks. A patron could pay a single entrance fee and occupy a seat for the whole day. But despite this, Bala found his natural courteousness intervened and he felt compelled to vacate a seat when he noticed newcomers standing. To add to his social skills he even took up ballroom dancing, surprising himself by winning a bronze medal for his dancing skills! In London he would spend many a weekend evening at the Hammersmith Palais Dance Hall.

In April 1950 they moved to London for a brief stint at the Regional Director's Office and then moved on to Southampton, the largest city and port on the southern coast of England, known for its old association with the RMS Titanic. He had already had some exposure to ocean-going mails while at the Fullerton but at Southampton he learnt how international mails were handled in accordance with the Universal Postal Convention. He would accompany the postal officer to the wharfs and then onward to the ocean-going steamers where mails were delivered and received.

The next stop for Bala and Clunies-Ross was Cardiff in Wales. Cardiff is yet another port city though the exposure that he had here would be of a different kind from Southampton. He would learn of the TPOs or the travelling post offices, which entailed the sorting of mails en route a mail train. The TPOs operated by the British Royal Mail formed a unique system wherein a railway carriage was fitted with a mail box so that letters could be posted while the train stood at a station. The sorting of the letters would be done by postal workers who were travelling in the train and the letters then delivered at subsequent stations of towns through which the train travelled. Bala marvelled at the efficiency of the system as the train started from Cardiff and moved to Cheltenham and then to Birmingham, where more postal workers joined them because of the large volume of mails they received. They would continue with the sorting till they reached Stoke where the Cardiff team disembarked and took the train home, again sorting through letters on the return journey which were to be delivered in Wales.

His stay in Wales was enjoyable. He found that the English speech there had a rhythm which to him appeared akin to spoken Tamil and the Welsh people were warm and friendly. While there he had the opportunity to participate in an *esteddfod*, the ancient Celtic tradition of celebrating poetry and music. He had discovered over the previous months that though the British were very cordial, they did not generally invite foreigners to their homes. However, it was in Shrewsbury that a Welsh family, the Lloyds, surprised him by inviting him to their home and he felt he had finally been able to get beyond the glass wall. In Cardiff he also took to paying regular visits to the British Council Hall. The café there provided fine meals at reasonable prices and he found he had the opportunity to meet students from other Commonwealth countries. A large number of them were from India but there was also a group from Singapore and Malaya and he was struck by how multiracial this group was. What surprised him even further was that unlike at home, here all the three nationalities of his country — the Chinese, Malays and Indians — came together with less inhibition. They met regularly to speak about the future of their country and this common thread of discussion united them together like never before. Despite the large number of Indians from India or other Commonwealth countries being present, Bala felt drawn by a new sense of comradeship to the young men from Singapore and returned again and again to this group and their common concern — the notion of a free Malaya. With no television and wartime censoring of newspapers, he knew little about the contemporary political scenario of India and what was happening in the subcontinent affected him even less. In contrast, he found the bond that tied him to his fellow Singaporeans to be far stronger and each time at the end of a meeting the group eagerly fixed an appointment for the time when they could meet again.

This sense of nationalism which unexpectedly dawned on Bala in a distant land can be connected to yet another incident which occurred in Wellington. Here he was invited by the Rotary Club to speak on Singapore. The Rotarians knew very little about this small island called Singapore and the Head Post Master persuaded Bala to accept the invite for a talk. Bala was caught unawares. He had no experience of public speaking, least of all to an English audience and yet could not turn down a senior official's request. He was fortunate to find a copy of Olaf Winstedt's *History of Malaya* handy, virtually the first scholarly work available on Malaya and written by the Oxford-educated civil servant. Bala made good use of the material and his talk went off well as evident in the request for a repeat performance at the Shrewsbury Polytechnic Institute. But the talk also left Bala a slightly changed person for a different reason. As he sat in his cold room in Shropshire reading up hurriedly about his homeland, he got to know his country better. He had virtually never had the opportunity to familiarise himself with Malaya's history, having given all his time to studying Britain, a pre-requisite of his school syllabus. Now as he read about Malaya he could not help but feel a sense of pride. Something stirred within him, a strong sense of connection and belonging, all the more emphasised perhaps by the strangeness of his surroundings.

The final stage of his UK scholarship took him to the administrative headquarter of the British Post Office in London. While there he took the opportunity to visit the Post Office Workers' Union in Dallington Street. He had been in touch with the body while he was in Singapore and now he visited the Union House Headquarters. He was warmly welcomed and given an insight into collaborative mechanisms for resolving working condition difficulties. What struck him at first was the difference in scale of activities between the Singapore and the UK unions. The UK union was far larger, commanding a support base of millions, yet they did not indulge in disruptive unionism. Instead they seemed to work in collaboration with the management and had their own Executive Committee, rather than being controlled by an external political party. Bala was invited to the Union's annual conference on the Isle of Man in May 1949. This was a time when the UPW (Union of Postal Workers) was headed by Charles Geddes and the impact of the

Union went far beyond the success of its strategy in wage negotiation. Geddes, on retiring as General Secretary of the Union had been nominated to the House of Lords, and it was he who invited Bala to participate in the conference. Subsequently, Geddes also invited him to come along as an Observer to the PTTI (Post, Telegraph & Telephone International) Conference to be held in Switzerland in July 1949 as well as the Scandinavian Conference to be held in Bergen in 1950. The Secretariat of the PTT Union was in Switzerland and at both the conferences French was the medium of communication. On reaching Switzerland Bala heard that the Singapore Union of P & T Workers had proposed that he should attend the conference as a Delegate rather than an Observer and he was requested to address the audience. He spoke briefly about the socio-political changes sweeping Singapore and his work with the postal union and his English speech was followed by a French translation. A timely nudge from his colleague told him that the applause that had broken out in the hall was for his speech, now rendered in French!

It was soon time to bid farewell to the UK. The two years of the scholarship programme were over and Bala felt he had lived an entire lifetime in that brief period. Nostalgic memories of Singapore and the Keppel Wharfs beckoned. In February 1951 he boarded the P & O Liner, *SS Canton* with his friend Clunies-Ross and they set sail, passing through the Suez Canal and touching the ports of Colombo and Penang, en route to the Far East.

Driving a Morris Minor in Communist-infested Country: Malaya

When Bala reported at the GPO the day after he reached Singapore, he was warmly welcomed by the Director of Posts, M L Durrant, but told that he would need to assume duty at the postal headquarters in Kuala Lumpur while Clunies-Ross would be posted at Penang since there were rules as per which returning candidates could not be posted in the same district where they had worked before their scholarship departure.

Incidentally, M L Durrant would soon initiate a scheme of "floating post offices" of red painted motor boats serving the neighbouring islands of Singapore.[11] And by 1952, Mobile Post Offices too would operate from vans to provide postal services to people in what was considered the rural areas of Singapore, i.e., Jurong, Sembawang, West Coast, Punggol, etc.

Thus, Bala found himself posted at the KL GPO, located in the expansive building of Mughal-eclectic architecture which houses parts of the Ministry of Information and Culture today.[12] The GPO was in the immediate vicinity of the Sultan Abdul Samad Building, facing the Selangor Club and Bala was appointed as a Cadet Assistant Controller of Posts here.

Bala found he was assigned to the Financial Division, the third critical arm of postal work (besides Administration and Postal Services) to which he had little exposure so far. It was an important posting and he would find the new learning would round him off and prepare him for the next senior position. In the Financial Division he was exposed to not only post office accounts and money orders but also to the important portfolio of the post office savings bank. The Post Office Savings Bank or the more prevalent present-day acronym, POSB, was established by the British in January 1877, as a means of providing banking opportunities to low income groups. The POSB's operations came under the jurisdiction of the Postmaster-General of the Straits Settlements and it proved to be one of the most popular saving banks started by the British Government with the number of accounts steadily increasing to 57,000 in 1940 with a total deposit of $14.3 million. The POSB was re-introduced during the Japanese period as a means of limiting the ever-spiralling inflation and various saving schemes were introduced with an apparently impressive result: the number of depositors in Syonan alone went up to 105,499 in July 1945. Subsequently after the return of the British, POSB's assets and liabilities were divided between Singapore and the FMS, though overall control remained in the hands of the Postmaster-General of Malaya, and between 1949 and 1955 the total deposit increased from $27.4

million to $57.6 million. The operations would be separated only after Singapore's independence in 1966 and the large volume of domestic savings that the POSB represented would be envisaged to play a key role in the island's industrialisation programme.

The exposure to the POSB operations proved to be enriching for Bala, enabling him to play a key role when in post-independent Singapore, Goh Keng Swee, the then Finance Minister, noting the potential of the scheme, formed the Savings Bank Committee. In April 1953, at the end of a year of post-scholarship probation period, Bala was confirmed as the Assistant Controller of Posts (ACP) of the Malayan Postal Service and posted to the Postal Central Division comprising the states of Selangor and Pahang. The Central Division was located in the GPO premises and formed the administrative headquarters of all the post offices of KL, the State of Selangor as well as some of the post offices of the State of Pahang and was headed by a Controller of Posts with two Assistant Controllers of Posts as his deputies. By all parameters it was a position of significance with a quantum leap in the range of responsibilities which Bala had handled when he left for the UK, and Bala felt justifiably elated by his posting. He, as one of the Assistant Controllers of Post, found he was responsible for the post offices of KL, which was a much bigger territory than the other states of the Federation forming the Central Division, as well as Selangor, while the other ACP was responsible for Pahang.

Thus after his return from the UK Bala started on a brand new segment of his career and the cordial relations which he had maintained with the senior officials helped him now. He had a good working relationship with the other Administrative Officers of the Central Division and of the Postal Headquarters in KL and was on first name terms with them. He soon found *Bala* became his improvised Christian name and he maintained contacts with Freddie Mack, the Assistant Controller of Posts, Singapore. Freddie Mack was no stranger to Singapore and Malaya, having been posted in the island as part of the British Army, and in fact had invited Bala and Clunies-Ross to his parent's home in Brighton while Bala was in Shrewsbury. He was in

England spending his furlong leave with his parents and had greeted Bala and Clunies-Ross as old acquaintances when he heard they hailed from Malaya. Bala also found he was on cordial terms with Bill Turner who had been one of his tutors at the Shrewsbury Postal Training Centre and Sammy Gammon who had been an Executive Officer in the British Post Office. It was Bala who had encouraged them to apply for appointments in the Malayan Postal Service and consequently, Sammy Gammon was now the Controller of Posts in Malaya. He also found David Smith, the Postmaster-General of Malaya, to be a kindly gentleman to whose residence he was invited for Christmas dinners. It was on David Smith's recommendation that as the Assistant Controller Bala was appointed the Secretary of the Postal Selection Committee meant for interviewing candidates for promotion to Higher Clerical Service as well as nominated to be the postal representative to the Federal Civil Service Staff Recruitment Committee of Selangor. Both these additional responsibilities were indicative of the faith the British senior officers placed in him.

But while his career prospects brightened, with the ongoing communist insurgency in Malaya he found his mortal life to be at considerable risk. Under the Emergency, the postal vans had police escort and postal agencies were set up in the larger of the *New Villages* or just outside to aid postal work. He realised how difficult it was for the communities in the *New Villages* to eke out a living, caught as they were between the communists and the British authority. Government accommodation was scarce and he had rented a wooden bungalow in the suburbs of Setapak, best known for three things — as a source of the Gombak River, as having hot springs and as a hideout for communists. The year was 1951 and though with the declaration of Emergency the British had been able to hold the insurgency in abeyance, they were still struggling to douse the fire completely and violent outbreaks occurred once in a while. The year 1949 had seen S A Ganapathy, the communist trade unionist and INA veteran, being hanged in Pudu Jail, despite requests of clemency from Indian leaders. In 1950 there had occurred an armed encounter between the Malaya police force and gunmen of the MCP (Malayan Communist Party) around the Bukit Kepong police station near Johor. And the subsequent year the British colonial administrator Sir Henry Gurney was murdered in cold blood by communists while he holidayed on Fraser's Hill in Pahang. Gurney had been deeply pessimistic of a truly "Malayan" consciousness ever emerging as opposed to a "Malay" one and one of the major British battles during the Emergency, other than extinguishing the communist fire, remained to foster a semblance of ethnic alliance in Malaya.

In Bala's time Kuala Semantan in Pahang remained a centre of MCP support and the Chin Peng-led MNLA (Malayan National Liberation Army), the successor of the MPAJA and yet another guerrilla force, took to launching exploratory raids on police stations and remote rural targets. Bala had arranged for his *amma* to come and look after him. She did all the marketing and reared poultry in the backyard, even striking up a friendship with Mrs Freddie Mack with Malay as their means of communication. But times were turbulent, the postal vans of Setapak needed police escorts and Bala found he was travelling to and from office by bus with a single journey taking almost an hour. Given the scarcity of new motor vehicles, Bala thought it prudent to apply for the purchase of a car. He was placed on a two-year wait list of a company which provided vehicles to government servants, and after a wait of almost a year, was the proud possessor of one — a Morris Minor purchased on an interest-free government loan. Next the problem of mastering the art of driving presented itself and fortunately, his friend Dorasamy came to his aid. He would visit Bala every Sunday, driving down for almost an hour from his residence in Pudu and soon with his lessons Bala had the confidence to take the Morris Minor to the roads. At that time Dorasamy was working as a higher clerical officer and it was their mutual interest in English literature which brought them close. Dorasamy or Dora introduced him to the pleasures of reading the *Rubaiyat of Omar Khayyam*, a book that Bala still holds close to his heart.

However, by 1954 it became increasingly evident that "Malayanisation" i.e., the process of replacing expatriate civil servants with Malayans in

Malaya and Singapore Officers in Singapore, was gathering strength. Several Officers from Singapore who had been posted in Malaya were recalled and in due course Bala too received directive and reported back to Singapore. Likewise, Clunies-Ross too was transferred back from Penang while two other Malayan officers trained in the UK and working in Singapore were released from duty and sent back to Malaya. Thus, in January 1955, Bala returned to Singapore after having spent nearly four years in KL and Selangor. During the time he had gained experience in various fields. He would make surprise inspection rounds of post offices and check the accounts and ensure the counter and delivery services were working efficiently. This experience in managing subsidiary post offices would help him in the future.

He returned to a postal service department in Singapore which had greatly expanded to meet the increasing demands. Now the department was led by a Director of Posts rather than the earlier Controller of Posts and the Director in turn was assisted by two Controllers of Posts instead of one and there were several Assistant Controllers of Posts. At first, Bala was appointed as head of the Registration and Parcel Branches and then moved, to be responsible for the work of all post offices and postal agencies on the island. There were over 30 post offices in the island and Bala as ACP found he was responsible for not only administrative and staffing matters, but also operational issues like controlling the delivery time, clearance of heavy mails during festive seasons as well as checking of postal accounts. He would pick any post office and arrive at the early hours without prior warning. Along with a hot cup of tea would arrive the cash box and the accounts of the previous day. As Bala reconciled the cash in hand of the post master, any misappropriation of funds would warrant a police case and arrest.

Controller of Posts: Singapore

Bala returned to a Singapore which seemed to have undergone a metamorphosis of sorts. When Bala had left for the UK in 1949 the Indian minority had enjoyed a certain prominence in Singapore politics. Their collective will to forge their own path in politics sprang from two rather contradictory emotions — a healthy dose of confidence after India's independence in 1947, peppered by a serious concern to consolidate their own future place as a minority in self-governing Singapore. Yet, during the interim period with the Emergency Regulations of 1948, the Registrar of Trade Unions was given the power to "freeze" the funds of a trade union if the elected union officer had disappeared and there was a second regulation which required the giving of notice before declaring a strike — both procedures aimed at preventing the labour movement going amiss. Restrictions had also been placed on meetings and associations, detention without trial was permitted and most leading communists had left Singapore for the Federation: urban revolution had obviously reached a dead end. The Communist Party had been proscribed, the communist-dominated SFTU disbanded and many of the leaders of the MNP arrested. The MDU or Malayan Democratic Union, an association of English-educated moderates towards which Bala and his friends had naturally gravitated, had dissolved itself in June 1948. And though the Singapore Labour Party was founded on the lines of the British Labour Party in September 1948, there was widespread scepticism about its leadership and no mass following had evolved.

Thus, the period following Bala's departure to the UK and then to Malaya had been marked by a bit of a void in Singapore's political scene. Former organisations had been dissolved and it was difficult for new ones to be formed. Unlike in Malaya, politics in Singapore remained non-communal with three clear ideological strains emerging — the radical communists, the conservative pro-British and the democratic socialists. While the communists were best represented by the MCP and the SFTU, the second group had as its political front the Progressive Party patronised by a group of prosperous, highly-westernised lawyers like John Laycock whose legal firm employed Lee

Kuan Yew. With the dissolution of the MDU democratic socialists like Bala who had supported multi-lingualism and democratic trade unions found themselves without a political party that they could ideologically endorse. While they were sympathetic towards objectives of social justice, they were inimical towards communist methods of armed revolution. On the other hand, an exposure to the INA and Subhas Chandra Bose ensured a pronounced anti-colonial stance which disallowed them from falling in with the Progressive Party. As a result when subsequently in November 1954, the People's Action Party (PAP) was formed by leaders like Lee Kuan Yew, S Rajaratnam and Goh Keng Swee, the group of trade unionists from government owned companies found the principles of democratic socialism that they espoused to be in full sympathy with their trade union interests and objectives. Consequently, at least seven out of the 14 founder members of the PAP were trade unionists and the party included familiar names like G Kandasamy, P Govindaswamy, A K Karuppiah and Ismail Rahim and Lee Gek Seng of the postal and telecommunication unions. Eventually, when the PAP contested the Legislative Council elections in 1955 and the City Council elections in 1957, these non-communist trade unionists helped considerably in mobilising electoral support.

Thus when Bala returned to Singapore, at first he encountered a political void and then the founding of the PAP in which many of his old friends were involved. However, as a Division I civil servant and government employee he thought it prudent to maintain a distance particularly as the year 1955 unfolded and proved to be one of dramatic change for Singapore. As the colonial system of administration was brought to the threshold of internal self-government, there was marked increase in the number of trade unions and industrial disputes. With the election of the Labour Government, trade unions took on a more militant stance and from April to September 1955 alone there were 214 strikes, the tension hitting a climax with the Hock Lee bus strike in which four were killed.

However, an invite to the XIV Universal Postal Union Congress in 1957 brought timely relief. Bala learnt he had been selected to join the Malayan delegation comprising Postmaster-General A S Gammon and Assistant Controller of Posts, Ong Keng Lian as a Singapore representative and that they were to attend the Congress to be held in Ottawa, Canada. It was later that he came to understand that his inclusion in the team had been made possible through a special request of the Singapore government, possibly because of the large volume of international mail handled by the island's postal service. Incidentally, the Universal Postal Union was established in 1874 and had soon emerged as the primary forum for international cooperation between the postal services of different countries and today it is a specialised agency of the UN based in Berne, Singapore.

Bala and the team flew to London and joined the British delegation as their Expert Attaches. The British delegation led by the Director of Postal Services R H Loke would first sail to Quebec and then travel by train to Ottawa where the Congress was to be held. Bala in haste had a dinner suit tailored from the clothing allowance approved for overseas travel. The Congress was held from 14th August to 3rd October 1957 in the Central Block of the Parliament Buildings in Ottawa. More than 350 delegates from 91 of the 96 member countries of the union participated with the Canadian Prime Minister, John Diefenbaker, giving the welcome address. The official language of the union remained French and all documents were published in French though English, Spanish and Russian were admitted as debating languages. The highlight of the Congress was the decision to establish the Consultative Committee for Postal Studies, a research wing dedicated to postal research. It was in Ottawa that Bala had an unforgettable encounter with the Canadian Liaison Officer, J L Delisle and forged yet another friendship which withstood the test of time. He also met one K Gopalakrishnan, a member of the Indian delegation and it was the latter who persuaded him to fly to Delhi. "It would be an enchanting and enlightening stopover," he chuckled and Bala would later realise that it had not been a vain persuasion!

Bala set sail from Canada even as the elm trees were turning crimson and while on the Atlantic he received an envelope marked to him from the KL Postal Headquarters — it was a letter from the Governor of Singapore informing him of his promotion to the position of Controller of Posts. The promotion was effective 1st April 1957 and the letter was predated to his departure to the Ottawa Congress. It was a joyous occasion indeed on the high seas, a high watermark of his career. On landing Bala decided to take his first overseas vacation. He would travel through continental Europe, stopping in India on the way back.

Conclusion

One of Bala's most lucid memories of his adolescence is when he would run around the Race Course of Singapore. In the evenings when he escorted his sisters to play in the open field he did not know how to kill time. Instead, he would simply join the runners there and circle the field, not very sure himself why he was doing so. One wonders how the transition happened from such an aimless existence to a life of dedicated purpose in his manhood. What were the triggers? Was it just coming of age and the responsibilities that he had to shoulder prematurely in his life? Or was his decision to take on a leadership role in the P & T Workers' Union the response of a man pushed back against a wall? It is true that the trade union movement of the post-war period was largely a response to the times. The dire economic situation, poor wages combined with a spiralling inflation made protest inevitable. But along with this was the political situation. For the trade unionists of the time, political and economic factors were necessarily intertwined. If the working conditions of the workers were to change then there needed to be a pro-labour government in power with a drive to build a fair and democratic society. And this awareness of what a fair society with an equitable distribution of wealth and power meant came from the politicisation they had undergone during the Japanese Occupation. With the INA Movement Bala had learnt it was possible to protest, to give vent to his resentment, in fact, that it was all right to feel resentment. And the confidence in his own capabilities came from the Japanese victory — it assured him of British fallibility as well as fostered a pride in Asian values. Even later in his life when he would travel to Japan for a conference he would appreciate their work culture — their diligence, polite modesty and respect for time.

The second question that arises is why Bala never thought of endorsing communism as an ideology of rebellion. As a member of the Malayan Democratic Union he and his peers had an equal exposure to Marxism as they did to socialism. How did he learn to distinguish between the two, particularly since in the initial days the communists were stronger and more vocal with the Singapore GLU and MCP as their frontal organisations? Anyway, whether a communist or a socialist, didn't the anti-colonial purpose remain the same? There is also an opinion that at this stage among the leftists, though there was a marked sympathy towards the communists, there were few who were doctrinaire Marxists. A political ideology was more of an identity marker which helped to unite, an amorphous notion of social justice and equality which helped to keep the masses together. In Bala's case perhaps the distinction mark between communists and socialists was clearer because the British were actively encouraging non-communist unions, which lent the movement an automatic legitimacy. Also, he is very emphatic in stating that he could not find it in himself to agree with the methods adopted by the communists. He had witnessed the MPAJA when they doled out summary justice in kangaroo courts and the vengeance with which they sought out those suspected of betraying their cause. Eventually, he would not condone their method of disruptive unionism either and would rather tread the path of nation-building advocated by the NTUC and PAP.

Besides the leadership role in the P & T Union, the other most critical incident of this period was Bala's sojourn to the UK on a scholarship and the Malayan nationalism that he felt burgeoning within him. Singapore was still torn up in its communal groups as far as nationalism was concerned and there was little stirring of emotions that an average Indian felt for Singapore or Malaya. Nehru's visit to Singapore in 1946 had merely reinforced the matriarchal ties to India. In fact, this was a period of some insecurity within the Indian community. Just as Indian independence had boosted the community's self-confidence, the subsequent partition had been an eye opener to the underlying violence in the country. Added to this was the Immigration Ordinance of 1952 which aimed to change the free port status of Singapore and impose immigration control. This, when combined with the call for a Malayan Union and the concurrent rise of Malay nationalism, painted a rather desultory picture for the future of the Indian community in Malaya. Some of the anxieties the minority community felt during these years find expression in R Jumabhoy's statements. In December 1952 he is vociferous in negating rumours that Indian clerks and merchants were leaving Malaya. Instead, he mentions, the departures were mainly labourers who intended to return. And again on 19th May 1953 while addressing the Legislative Council he speaks of the Federation of Malaya which if seeking to attain a self-government status needed to base their "politics on a Malayan-born basis" and not on a communal basis. He goes on to mention that communal parties like the MCA and UMNO had no business to speak about self-government; there were other lesser communities like the Indians, Ceylonese and Eurasians but the Indians held the "balance of power".[13]

So given the circumstances, what generated the Malay nationalism in Bala? That too in far off Shrewsbury, while perhaps munching on a ham and cheese sandwich in the British Council Café? Part of it was of course his multiracial childhood, the Malay and Chinese friends with whom he had played since childhood and the *Melayu Pasar* or Bazaar

Malay which he had learnt to speak. In a foreign land he found there were natural bonds which he formed with the Chinese and Malays who had travelled from Singapore or Malaya. The ties cut through the communal identities which had seemed all-important before and instead the common problems they faced and needed to find a solution to once they returned held them together. Part of it was his reading of Winstedt's *History of Malaya*, his first exposure to his own country's history and the ancient ties that he discovered which had tied India to Southeast Asia. With time he would read about the Buddhist Srivijaya Empire and of the tales of valour of the King of Ligor, which had found their way on a stone plaque all the way in Nagapattinam in Tamil Nadu. He discovered it was a shared past which went back for centuries based on spiritual and cultural exchange and his presence in Malaya was not a mere coincidence dictated by commercial concerns of the British.

Along with these factors, ironically enough, another trigger to his Malay nationalism were the British themselves. Subhas Chandra Bose when he had travelled to Cambridge had written,

> Whether one wills it or not, the climate of this country makes people energetic. The activity you see here is most heartening. Every man is conscious of the value of time and there is a method in all that goes on…Students here have a status — and the way the professors treat them is different.[14]

It was the same for Bala. Like Bose, it was the first time he breathed the air of a free country and it made him realise the value of freedom. He noticed how, despite wartime difficulties, the English stood in queues for their food ration, the fervour with which they protected their past, the pride they took in their own culture and this inspired him. He returned not only having learnt the regulations of the British Post Office but with a new work ethic — serving the country also meant maintaining discipline and dedication to the job at hand.

The next big question that arises is why Bala did not decide to go back to trade unionism on his return from KL. 1954–55 was a time when the Rendel Constitution warranted a more relaxed political environment in Singapore and saw a revival of the leftist movement. The radicals were now fighting not only for better wages but for associated causes like arbitrary dismissals, detention of their leaders and strikes to express sympathy to other unions as well. The reason why Bala refrained was of course partially because of his seniority on the corporate ladder but one also wonders if he felt by this time and during the subsequent years the trade union movement had become too deeply politicalised. The unions enjoyed a large following and would be increasingly used to add weight to political parties — be it the Progressive Party or the PAP. Bala also confides that as a former unionist he continued to be under the radar. In 1954 an incident occurred which emphasised this: Bala was in KL when he heard his old friend Kandasamy was leaving for Oxford to study industrial relations at the Ruskin College on an UNESCO Fellowship. Bala decided to travel to Singapore to bid him farewell and spent the weekend at his parents' government quarters at Towner Road. However, the news of his private visit reached the ears of the KL Postmaster-General and the next day he was summoned to David Smith's office. He was told in no uncertain terms that during his visit to the AUPE General Secretary's residence the uniformed postal staff union had served a notice for strike and now the department was hard-pressed to prepare confidential plans to deal with the situation. Though Bala's explanations were accepted and he could leave David Smith's office without apprehension, he got the distinct feeling that in the future too his movements and associations would be watched and that as a senior civil servant he was required not to be involved in any political movement.

Notes

[1] Article quoted from *Telepost* in *Singapore Free Press*, 16 January 1948.

[2] Article quoted from *Telepost* in *Straits Times*, 15 April 1948.

[3] *Not by Wages Alone: Selected Speeches and Writings of C.V. Devan Nair, 1959–1981*, C V Devan Nair. NTUC, Singapore, 1982.

[4] The postal union initially comprised Divisions 2, 3 & 4 of the staff which consisted of the white collar clerical staff, the higher division clerks, the superintendents as well as the blue collar uniformed staff.

[5] Some details of the postal union taken from *Public Service Unionism: A History of the AUPE in Singapore*, R K Vasil. Times Book International, Singapore, 1979.

[6] *An Unexpected Journey: Path to the Presidency*, S R Nathan. EDM Books, Singapore, 2011, pp. 133–34.

[7] *Not by Wages Alone*, p. 86.

[8] *Straits Times*, 20 April 1948.

[9] *Singapore Free Press*, 20 August 1947.

[10] Details of the time-scale pay plan in the *Straits Times*, 20 April 1948.

[11] *Straits Times*, 27 June 1956. The floating post offices were to provide a daily shuttle service to Tanjong Kling, Pulau Simakan, St John's Island and Blakang Mati.

[12] The GPO moved out from this building in 1984.

[13] MCA = Malayan Chinese Association; UMNO = United Malays National Organisation.

[14] *An Indian Pilgrim: An Unfinished Biography*, Subhas Chandra Bose. Eds. Sisir Kr Bose and Sugata Bose. Netaji Collected Works, Vol. 1. Oxford University Press, New Delhi, 1997, p. 168, letter of 26 August 1919.

December 1948. Post Office Union members and friends bid Bala farewell on his scholarship to the UK at the quay at Tanjong Pagar. In 2016, Bala received this photo via email from Lee Khee Wee in London, an industrious colleague who became an intimate friend. *First row, right: G Kandasamy. Second row, fourth from left: Kanesan. Third row: Bala and Lee Khee Wee.*

1948. Bala with committee members of the Singapore Union of P & T Workers. This was a farewell photo taken at the P. O. Club in Serangoon Road. *Sitting. Second from left: G Kandasamy. Fourth from left: Bala.*

1949. Bala attends the PTTI (Post, Telegraph, Telephone International) Conference in Switzerland.

1950–1951. Bala in London with Clunies-Ross and Kartar Singh.

1950–1951. Training in London with Ong Keng Lian from Penang.

1952. A social gathering of senior expatriate postal officers. *Front table, left: Mr and Mrs Kartar Singh. Bala is seated at the extreme right.*

1952. A group photo taken at the same gathering of senior expatriate postal officers. *Standing. First row, left-most: Selvarajoo. Third from left: Clunies-Ross. Second and third rows, centre: Mr and Mrs Kartar Singh. Standing behind Kartar Singh (on his left) is Bala.*

1954. Director of Posts, A S Gammon inspecting the letter sorting with a dignitary.

1956. Bala at the GPO as the Assistant Controller of Posts.

1956. Social gathering at badminton hall on Guillemard Road, Singapore. Bala dances the *ronggeng*. In the background is Lee Kuan Yew.

Chapter 5

Restore this Sun to us and the Waiting Generations

Post-War, Independence: 1957–1971

"We do but merely ask, no more, no less,
This much: that you white man, boasting
Of many parts, Some talk of Alexander
Some of Hercules…
We ask you see the bitter, curving tide of history,
See well enough, relinquish, restore this place,
This sun to us…and the waiting generations.
Depart white man."

May 1954, Singapore
— Edwin Thumboo

On the Malayanisation Chessboard

The results of the April 1955 General Elections came as a bit of a surprise to the British. Turnbull calls it's the first lively political contest in the history of Singapore. Bala remembers it as a time when political parties had sprung up, there were many political rallies and lunch-time meetings at the Empress Place and Fullerton Square were well attended. The surprise element was the fact that 'spirited competition' did not come from the two biggest electoral competitors — the Progressive and Democratic Parties but instead from comparative newbies — the People's Action Party and the Labour Front — both of which were radical, managed to stir mass sentiments with their campaigning and attracted large numbers of Chinese voters. Though the PAP fielded only a token of four candidates in protest against the Rendell Constitution and the Labour Front only 17, it was increasingly apparent that the future belonged to them.

The David Marshall-led Labour Front campaigned hard to build mass support and one of the key issues in their election manifesto, along with seizing immediate self-government for a merged Singapore and Malaya, was the demand for a Malayanisation of the Public Administration within the next four years. This meant that once the Labour Front formed the minority left-wing government, they were quick to activate the Malayanisation process: the Malayanisation Committee was established under the chairmanship of the eminent doctor, B R Sreenivasan, who in 1948 was a founder-member of the Singapore Anti-Tuberculosis Association and would later be the Vice-Chancellor of the University of Singapore. By December 1956, the Legislative Assembly of Singapore also accepted the Malayanisation Committee's report, which advocated the localisation within two years of general administrative posts of the public service and the remaining professional posts within four years. By 1957, a Public Service Commission with full executive powers would be set up and Malayanisation would proceed rapidly.

But even as the process unfolded the first pinpricks of problems made themselves apparent. Thus, on 4th June 1956, there was David Marshall writing to the colonial office saying that perhaps the Committee was being a bit too "over-optimistic" in terms of not only the timetable but also in not considering the impact that a "large-scale exodus of expatriate officers" would have.[1] From the same period there is yet another Memorandum from the Chief Secretary on the problems of transferring staff between the Malayan Federation and Singapore as a part of the Malayanisation process.[2] According to it, the process was rapidly getting too cumbersome and leading to delays in filling up critical vacancies. Besides it was increasingly unacceptable to both the governments that the transferred officers should swell the numbers of 'entitled officers' under the compensation schemes designed for this purpose.[3]

As the Malayanisation scheme fell into place across sectors of public service there were other issues which came to light. There was a dearth of suitably professionally qualified senior officers, which meant that probationary assistants had to be quickly locally recruited, keeping in mind that they would be needed to be trained so that they could take over senior positions in three to four years. The future careers of senior expatriate officers needed to be planned keeping in mind that they would need to transit within a specified period of time and local officers needed to be attached to them as an understudy so that the transition would be smooth. The required training in the UK needed to be planned since the normal gestation period between recruitment and professional qualification itself was likely to be three to four years. But perhaps the issue which warranted the most heated of debates was that of compensation — the payment of superannuation and provident fund to senior expatriate officers.

But even as such questions and controversies kept the Malayanisation Commission busy, one wonders what was happening in the postal department of Singapore where Bala was now attached. By January 1955, he had returned to Singapore from Malaya and was working as an ACP or Assistant Controller of Post. That Malayanisation was to soon impact the postal department and that the excitement levels were rapidly building up, is apparent in one of the early articles in the *Straits Times*. On 19th June 1955 there appears an article titled *Posties to get Top Jobs*, which mentions the Postmaster-General E E Cassell's comment (Cassell was previously Regional Director, P & T, East Africa and had succeeded David Smith as Postmaster-General, Malaya in 1954) to the Post Officer Workers' Union that it was a part of his job to find someone locally who could eventually take his position and adds that "personality, judgement and administrative ability" were needed for Division 1 jobs. Advancement was to become extremely competitive and only the best would get higher posts. Again on 14th June 1956 there is mention of the Malayanisation Committee's decision that non-professional public service departments could be Malayanised with immediate effect, with no discernible loss of efficiency and such departments included postal, information, social welfare and registration — a fact that would obviously auger well for Bala. A more detailed plan for the postal department appears by the end of the same year: on 3rd December 1956 the *Straits Times* speaks of the Malayanisation Commission's acceptance of the Postmaster-General's proposal that Malayanisation of the entire department would take approximately four years with the retention period of Directors being three years, Controllers two years and of ACPs till the end of their temporary period of transfer with no promotion prospects.[4] Another issue pertaining to the postal department which finds repeated mention is the question of training postal officers in the British Post Office. Thus in 1954 there is mention of the Postmaster-General's comment that the department had tried promoting senior clerical officers of the Clerical Superscale to be Assistant Controllers of Post but the experiment had been unsatisfactory since the "officers, after promotion, still remain basically Office Assistants." As a solution he felt that a period of training with the British Post Office helped them gain in confidence and gave them "that ability to take the initiative which was necessary if they were to carry the responsibilities of a Division 1 officer."[5]

Thus, perhaps unknown to Bala, forces were coming together and decisions were being taken which finally would facilitate his taking over as Controller of Posts on 1st April 1957. As a Controller he would be head of Operations while C D Clunies-Ross, his old friend and counterpart would head Administration with Low Siow Chek (ACP — Administration: General & Personnel), Choo Koh Eng (ACP — Administration: Accounts & Stores), G Rajendram (ACP — Development & Planning), Wong Lee Hoong (ACP — Investigation), Kartar Singh (ACP — Mails), G Kandasamy (ACP — Parcels & Registration), Ismail Abdul Hamid (ACP — Sub Post Office & Postal Agency) and Boey Khye Leng (ACP — Airport & forces PO) under them. Subsequently, on 19th May 1958 the last British Director of Posts, H M Rose, would retire to the UK and Bala would take over as Acting Director of Posts with Clunies-Ross and Kartar Singh reporting to him as Controllers of Post. Till 1965 and Singapore's independence, he would continue to report to the Postal Headquarters in Malaya, first to Postmaster-General A S Gammon and then to PMG Eric Montague May. While Bala would be Director of Posts (DOP) for Singapore, there would be similar DOPs from the Malayan Federation and Straits Settlement reporting to the PMG. Once Bala took on the responsibility, he attempted not only to continue the quality of public service provided by the post office department but also to enhance it: the department would take on the additional responsibility of paying government pensions as well as special retirement benefits to retrenched local staff. Besides, during this time annual awards were institutionalised for the recognition of sub-post offices which excelled on four counts — delivery, counter services, accounts and the general upkeep of the offices. *Rain or Shine, the mail must go through* remained their motto.

Thus on 27th July 1958, soon after Bala's taking over as DOP, the *Straits Times* quotes PMG A S Gammon as saying that he felt confident that the postal department of Singapore would be in "safe hands" after Malayanisation. Addressing the annual delegates' conference of the

Union of Postal Workers, he mentions that the department has only 10 expat officers remaining and the target of complete Malayanisation would be met, as scheduled, by end 1960 to which Acting Minister of Works, Posts and Telecommunication, Inche Abdul Rahman bin Talib (later Minister of Education) agreed readily, expressing his delight at the speed with which Malayanisation was proceeding in the postal department. Subsequent to Singapore's independence, with additional responsibilities falling on the shoulders of the postal department, Clunies-Ross would be appointed as Deputy Postmaster-General to Bala. But with Clunies-Ross's early retirement in 1971, it would be Wong Lee Hoong, yet another of Bala's trusted friends and colleagues who would succeed Bala as PMG once Bala too retired in 1971. Incidentally, Wong Lee Hoong along with Low Siow Chek was the first of the postal employees to be recruited directly from the university and following them, the same practice of recruitment would be followed for all administrative officers. Thus, after Bala, the good work of the postal department would continue with changes introduced as and when required. In the year 1979, Singapore's postal code would be changed from a two-digit to a four-digit number to cater to the needs of an expanding population and on 1st September 1995, the current six-digit postal code would be introduced with the first two numbers representing the sector and the remaining four indicating the delivery point within the sector. This mailing system would drastically reduce manual sorting. Today, the corporate headquarters of Singapore Post has moved out of the Fullerton Building and is located in a state-of-the-art mail processing centre called Singapore Post Centre (SPC) in Paya Lebar.

Bala's taking over as the DOP of Singapore was the final approbation of his work and professionalism of over two decades. Yet on hindsight it is interesting to note how carefully Providence had guarded his way, one false turn and perhaps his life could have taken on a very different look. The first of course was his decision in 1945 to not join the Singapore Telecommunication Department but to continue with the Mails Branch of the postal department. This proved to be fortunate for with Malayanisation it was decided that only qualified electrical engineers would be considered for promotion to officer level in the Telecommunication Department.[6] The second was when he and Clunies-Ross were selected to return from Malaya to Singapore as a part of the Malayanisation process in January 1955. Fortunately the official decision came just before the trend swung to the other side and it was decided that exchanging officers between Singapore and the Malayan Federation was becoming increasingly cumbersome. The third was him being chosen for training under the British Postal system. He and Clunies-Ross and subsequently Wong Lee Hoong, Low Siow Chek, G Kandasamy, Kartar Singh and G Rajendram would comprise the batches which were sent to the UK for training. With the PAP coming to power in 1959 there would be renewed control on this policy as a measure of cost cutting and such postal training in the UK would be stopped. But Bala would maintain that it was his training stint in the UK which gave him the confidence to handle the DOP's job.

But that such rapid Malayanisation of key departments was not being looked upon too kindly by certain factions of the society was also soon becoming apparent. Thus by 1959 letters started appearing in the *Straits Times* which questioned the fact that too many Indians seemed to be taking up the top jobs: was the process to be called "Asianisation" or "Malayanisation"? And even earlier there was concern expressed by the Malay League that the question of nationality needed to be solved first, till then there was need to take Malayanisation at a cautious speed. The same League would continue to demand passport regulation between Singapore and the Federation until the merger of the two territories was an established fact. The regulation was felt to be important for protecting the interest of the Malays and the League felt that with the rapid increase of non-Malay population in Singapore and with them travelling to the Federation, there was a possibility that the Malays of the Federation would finally be outnumbered.[7]

By 1959 Singapore was heading for yet another major change. The path that was being carved out for Singapore had already diverged from that of Malaya. While David Marshall's minority government faced stiff opposition from Lee Kuan Yew's PAP, in Malaya Tunku Abdul Rahman's political party won a landslide victory and by 1957 Malaya was announced to be a fully independent state. In Singapore the 'men in white' came to power after GE 1959 and it was only subsequently that Singapore became fully self-governing. Self-government brought with it a whole new approach to life as the led became leaders, the ruled became rulers and the unfulfilled dream became a fulfilled reality. For Bala too, life was to take yet another turn as having achieved much more than he had envisaged in his profession, he set out to broaden his horizons and return to his community some of what he had gleaned in the last 42 years.

Life is Pleasant …Sometime Not So

Though in the 1950s anti-British sentiments were at a peak, judging by the size of the crowds which gathered at the Clifford Pier to welcome HRH the Duke of Edinburgh, the British royalty obviously continued to be a major draw. Prince Philip visited Singapore from the 22nd to the 24th of February 1958 and reportedly a crowd of nearly 200,000 people gathered and enthusiastically cheered as the Prince entered the Constitutional Exposition grounds at the Kallang Basin. He had arrived in the royal yacht *Britannia* and had been welcomed by Sir William Goode, the last British Governor of Singapore as well as the then Chief Minister and successor to David Marshall, Tun Lim Hew Hock.

The Prince set sail from the Clifford Pier in a launch and arrived at the fair site at the Constitutional Exposition grounds at around 10.25 in the night. The lateness of the hour was not a deterrent and there was a huge crowd waiting in the fairgrounds as the Prince was welcomed by members of the fair committee. He was introduced to MP and Chairman of the coordinating committee for the government pavilion,

M P D Nair, and walked down the wide ally formed by a long line of police to hold back the crowd that had been waiting for several hours to see him. Despite the enthusiastic crowd which threatened to break through the cordon, the entourage walked at a steady pace as they were already running behind schedule for the reception planned later in the night. Bala was at the Singapore Post Office stall which was a part of the Government Pavilion and to his surprise M P D Nair had pre-arranged for the entourage to pause at the Post Office stall and thus it so happened that Bala, for the first time in his life, had the opportunity to be introduced to royalty. It was only later that he got to know that Mr Nair had specially requested Bala's presence at the exposition.

An encounter that was not pleasant in equal measure followed the next year. This was with former Mayor, Ong Eng Guan. After the General Elections of 1959 in which the PAP won a landslide victory, the postal department came under the purview of Ong Eng Guan, i.e., the Minister of National Development. This was following the controversy regarding the Singapore City Council in July 1959 after which the PAP absorbed the Council into the central government and the days of municipal democracy were decidedly over. Most City Council functions, including the supervision of the Harbour Board and Housing Board, were transferred to the Ministry of National Development and Ong Eng Guan was assigned this key ministry and was also appointed as one of the three Singapore members on the influential Internal Security Council. He was reputed to be a bitter anti-colonialist and as Mayor of the Municipal Council was said to have dismissed staff members at will.

Now, soon after his appointment as Minister, he summoned heads of all government departments of his ministry. Bala attended the meeting at his office in Upper Pickering Street. Among other things, he warned that department heads must ensure that the staff worked diligently and that he would not tolerate queues at public counters. Bala, following the tradition of the British Postal Service, was proud of the service his department provided to the public. He felt he and his team had taken every possible step to avoid inconveniencing the public at post office counters but during lunch time and office closing time, queues at the GPO and other post offices were unavoidable — a feature common even at post offices in other parts of the world.

Bala, thus felt he should take the opportunity to explain the reasons for the unavoidable queues seen at times at the post offices. However, the minister was visibly annoyed at his interjection and curtly remarked that counter clerks should work diligently as their work was as simple as issuing tickets at cinemas. Bala, protective of his team, rose to reply. He wished to say that even at cinemas at times queues were not uncommon but held himself in check when the expatriate permanent secretary signalled him to sit down and the meeting continued with other matters. For Bala it was a valuable lesson learned — he realised not only was it wiser at times to let discretion get the better of valour, but that whether a fellow Asian or English, he needed to exercise caution when interacting with a politician in public.

Bala remembers this period for yet another momentous event — he joined the Singapore Indian Association (SIA) in 1960. The SIA had been founded in 1923, one of the oldest of Indian bodies in Singapore, with its premises in Short Street and tennis courts and a playing field in Balestier Road.[8] The first President had been Mohamed Haji Dawood who had settled in Singapore, though originally from Surat, India. Later, individuals like A C Chander, a Bengali and the famous philanthropist, R Jumabhoy, had taken over the presidential chair. In the 1920s the Association had been at its peak and functioned as a mouthpiece of the Indian community with dignitaries from the subcontinent regularly invited and lavishly entertained on its premises. Subsequently, during the 1930s the SIA went through one of its lowest ebbs as intercommunal discord and provincialism took its toll on its leadership. It was only after the war and with R Jumabhoy's return from India in 1945 that the Association was revived with its temporary premises in Race Course Road. Subsequently, the foundation stone of the present premises in Balestier Road was laid by Indian Prime

Minister Jawaharlal Nehru when he came to Singapore in 1950. In 1954, Vijaylakshmi Pandit, Nehru's sister, laid the foundation stone for the extension of the building incorporating the main hall.

Bala's association with the SIA began in 1960 when he applied and became a member. His friend Freddie Fernandez was an enthusiastic tennis convener and he talked him into taking up the game which was entirely new to Bala. His offer to provide coaching free of charge proved irresistible and Bala ventured into the sport. Freddie arranged practice sessions on Sunday mornings at the SIA tennis courts and Bala's skills soon improved and he began to enjoy playing tennis as a partner in a doubles game. It was during such practice sessions that he got to know G Ramachandran, who was later to become the President of the Indian Chamber of Commerce in 1966 and a Trustee of the Indian Association in 1980.

Soon Ramasamy P, the Secretary of the Association, persuaded Bala to join the Management Committee and he was elected the Vice President when Balbadhar Singh took over as President in 1962. In 1964 Bala would become the President himself on the proposal of the outgoing President Balbadhar Singh and remain in office for four consecutive years till 1968 — some of the most crucial years in the history of Singapore. As Singapore first merged with Malaya in 1963 and then became a sovereign nation in 1965, national cohesion based on a multi-racial secular society emerged as one of the important aims of the government. Bala would keep this larger picture in mind while steering affairs of the Association and he, along with the Management Committee, decided to commemorate local events of importance like the National Day rather than only Indian occasions and festivals.

Bala's involvement with the Hindu Endowments Board, a statutory board under the Singapore government, also began in the early 1960s while he was DOP, Singapore. His old friend and postal colleague G Kandasamy was elected to the Legislative Assembly in 1959 and became the Parliamentary Secretary of Culture the subsequent year. He took under his wing the affairs of the Muslim and Hindu Endowments Boards and persuaded Bala to join him in the work he had undertaken of improving the organisational infrastructure and rebuilding of the Hindu temples. Bala became a member of the Board in 1961 and continued to hold the appointment until the repeal of the Muslim and Hindu Endowments Boards in 1969. Subsequently when the newly constituted Hindu Endowments Board came into operation in 1969, he continued to serve on the Board till 1972 as well as serve as the Chairman of the Hindu Advisory Board from 1972 to 1974 which acted as a consulting body for any doubts and queries about Hinduism.

As a member of the Hindu Endowments Board, Bala became deeply involved in the rebuilding of the Sri Sivan and Sri Srinivasa Perumal temples of Singapore. He was the Chairman of the Sivan temple which had been built in 1850 though the site was used for temple worship as far back as in 1821. The Perumal Temple was also one of the early temples built in 1860 and both had over the years fallen into disrepair and were in need of urgent renovation. Further, there was a need for a suitable hall for Hindus to conduct marriages and social functions.

Consequently, the Sivan and Perumal Temples Building Fund Committee was established in 1961 with Kandasamy as Chairman and Bala as Secretary. Collection of funds was started with enthusiasm but the response was weak. The timely $50,000 given by the City Council as compensation for the Sivan Temple land acquired for widening of Orchard Road came in very handy.

Work on the construction of the Sivan Temple was started in 1961 but progress was slow. However, a sub-committee was appointed in May 1964 which supervised and expedited the completion of the project. The final consecration ceremony was performed on 9th December 1964 in the presence of Minister of Social Affairs and famous former Malay journalist, Inche Othman Bin Wok. According to municipal records the first consecration of the Sivan Temple was held in 1905: a singular phase of reconstruction work started in this temple premises in 1898 with a plan entitled, "Rebuild Hindu Sivan Temple in Orchard Road" submitted by a municipal engineer, S Tomlinson (Plan # 19/1898, CBS 337, National Archives).[9] The reconstruction work took several years to complete with V Nagappa Chetty and his wife providing most of the funds. During the reconstruction work a stone inscription was discovered which stated that the temple site was worshipped at even the year 1821, making it the oldest Hindu temple of Singapore. The final consecration of the rebuilt temple was held on 9th February 1905 and now as Bala supervised the reconstruction work and consecration ceremony again after nearly 60 years, it was truly as though history had completed a full circle and he was witness to it.

Life is Pleasant…Sometime Not So…Continued

The early 1960s was a time of rapid changes in Singapore and Malaya. Even as Singapore was taking bold steps in self-government and the PAP-led government undertook what Lee Kuan Yew at the time of assuming office in 1959 had called "a social revolution by peaceful means", there was trouble brewing in other quarters. Lee Kuan Yew had gained considerable success in negotiating a highly favourable agreement for Singapore in the Malaysia merger and the Federation of Malaysia was scheduled to come into being on 31st August 1963.[10] But the Tunku of Malaysia deferred the implementation of the same because of objections from President Sukarno of Indonesia who criticised the Malaysian concept as a "neo-colonialist plot" since it thwarted his dream of uniting the Malay countries. Consequently and despite the Tunku's best efforts to convince him, Sukarno would decide to launch an armed confrontation against the newly formed Federation in 1963 which would eventually last for three years and go under the term Konfrontasi.

Bala recalls an interesting incident from the period of Konfrontasi. An English Missionary arrived at the Singapore Airport with a dozen or more letters addressed to Singapore residents. He was detained by customs officials for infringing postal regulations. In the normal course he could be charged in the law court and fined for exceeding the prescribed limit of letters allowed to be personally carried by a passenger into Singapore, such privilege being the preserve only of the postal administration of the country of origin. The Missionary was brought to Bala's office and explained that he was acting merely as a free of charge carrier since letters sent through the Indonesian postal service appeared not to have reached the anxious addressees for some months. Bala felt sympathetic towards the difficulties of the times and had him released on payment of the local postage fees for transmission of the letters through Singapore post.

Even while the Konfrontasi was going on, Bala attended a seminar on postal service from 1st February to 6th February 1964 in Tokyo. Heads and senior administrative officers from Southeast Asian countries as well as India and Pakistan attended the talks. The seminar was conducted by lecture sessions followed by onsite visits to the Japanese Postal Headquarters and Post Offices.

During his visit to Japan, Bala got the opportunity to observe the Post Office Savings Bank (POSB) of Japan — an experience which would prove valuable to him very soon. He realised in Japan the POSB was organised more like a full-fledged business or a commercial bank providing monetary services and was spread extensively throughout the country. The Savings Bank offices were established in separate premises and with fulltime canvassers employed in mobilising new depositors and increased quantum of deposits. It was actually a successful enterprise and one of the leading banking institutions. Bala felt it was a unique system to suit the Japanese way of life.

He also noticed how far the Japanese had progressed in mechanising the handling of letters and parcels and found the process very impressive. The daily number of parcels handled at the GPO was so large it would have been uneconomical to employ manual labour and find additional operation rooms. Stamp cancelling machines and extensive conveyor belt methods were used for the handling of large volume of postal articles and research was being conducted in the field of letter sorting machines. Bala realised while Singapore was already using letter cancelling machines, the use of letter and parcel machines could definitely be a matter of future consideration.

During weekends the participants of the conference were taken on cultural tours and Bala was once again impressed with the city as well as the Japanese people's way of life. One such evening he was invited for a dinner with some of his Japanese colleagues and to his immense pleasure discovered that they had been to Malaya during the period of Japanese Occupation and now were continuing their disrupted postal career in Japan. One Mr Hakozaki who had been his colleague in KL had come to know of Bala's participation in the seminar and had organised the function. There were nearly 10 men in the group and Bala knew many of them and it turned out to be a bitter-sweet evening as they sadly reminiscenced about the past and yet looked to the future with new hope and happiness. While the evening was in progress Bala could with ease find the whereabouts of his old friend, Akifuji, and later one of the seminar officers organised not only his train journey but also provided him with an official who would escort him to Akifuji's residence. He was graciously welcomed by his friend who very kindly organised his stay at a hotel nearby — though luxurious, Bala, a man bred in tropical climes found the room to be too cold!

This was a time of severe racial tensions in Singapore as the merger with Malaysia was hotly debated and the PAP challenged the UMNO (United Malays National Organisation) in the March 1964 Malaysia Federal Elections. The underlying tensions soon found an outlet and ethnic riots broke out in two separate incidents during 1964 — one in the month of July allegedly incited by the ultra-nationalists of the Singapore wing of UMNO pressing for special privileges for the Malays, and the other in September when a Malay trishaw-puller was attacked and killed by a group which was believed to be ethnic Chinese. Bala, who was now the senior-most postal official in Singapore, had through the years managed to maintain a cordial relationship with the P & T Unions which he had himself been instrumental in creating. The Whitley Departmental Joint Committee which had been established almost 10 years ago was still functioning well and helped keep worker-employer relations on an even keel.

However, during this period he was entangled in a serious problem with the Union: an article in the Union Newsletter expressed in rather uncomplimentary terms the arrangements made by postal authorities in sending the delivery postmen after work to the Geylang area during the racial riots of July 1964. Bala, justifiably upset since he had been personally present during the whole episode and had ensured the safety of the concerned workers, spoke to Kandasamy, the Secretary of the AUPE (Amalgamated Union of Public Employees) who quickly organised a meeting with the authors of the concerned article. Bala in turn accepted the writers' apology and in the following issue of the newsletter the authors' expressed their apology and unreservedly withdrew the offending article.

Thereafter Bala's relationship with the Union was never disrupted. To strengthen the contact with Union leaders he made it a point to invite them to the Deepavali dinner he organised at his residence every year. He would also invite senior officers to enable them to establish social contact with worker representatives.

The first half of the 1960s was thus a period when Bala could reap some of the benefits of the hard work he had devoted to his career. It was also a time of spreading his wings when he ventured into social and community work and found it gave him a rare satisfaction. Despite political upheavals in the background, life seemed to be progressing with a steadiness that was new to Bala since war broke out in Singapore. Yet, perhaps unknown to him destiny had other plans — life was to take yet another sharp turn soon and he was soon to discover there was much more to life than work!

Pleasures of Independence, Pleasures of Bondage

Independence came as a surprise to Singapore. A sovereignty separate from Malaysia had not been envisaged by the members of the PAP or indeed any other responsible politician of Singapore. The island depended on the Federation of Malaysia for water, for trade, perhaps even for survival and such a separation was inconceivable. In fact for many years to come Singapore's dependence on Malaysia for water would be seen as one of the most tangible signs of its vulnerability and it would take over four decades to create the high-grade recycled NEWater — a turning point in Singapore's history after which many felt Singapore was truly set free.

No Singaporean can remember the day of independence in 1965 without thinking of two things — the sense of shock that ran through society at being unceremoniously ousted within just two years of joining the Federation, and Lee Kuan Yew's emotional outburst at the press conference of 9th August 1965, the long pauses as he struggled for self-control while speaking of the separation. Later when asked that according to Malaysia the obsession with Malaysia was his, that they were less obsessed with Singapore, he would reply, "No, but we have not said anything that displayed obsession. We just kept our thoughts to ourselves."[11]

But even while Singapore reeled under the blow, for a while the PAP continued to contemplate of Singapore being re-admitted to the Federation, Malay continued as the national language and a Muslim, Yusof bin Ishak became the republic's first President. However, the civilian citizens showed an apparent calm. In fact after the initial confusion Bala too felt a sense of relief because he felt the separation might herald a time of peace and the racial tensions might abate.

For Bala the independence of Singapore and the severance of ties with Malaysia meant, as it did to other senior officials of the public service, a much larger gamut of responsibilities fell his way. It was decided that with independence, Singapore would opt out of the Malayan Postal Union Agreement and all Singapore-related work would be transferred back to Singapore from the postal headquarters at KL. A budget of $1 million was approved for the project and it proved to be a mammoth task. The three major departments which needed to be moved back were record keeping including not only personal records of all postal employees but also postal pass books of all customers from Singapore, the finance department as a whole including financial books and ledgers and the entire set up and records for the POSB. And the transfer needed to happen overnight!

Keeping the forthcoming possibility of shortage of space in the Fullerton Building in mind, new space was acquired: an old government bungalow in the Tanglin Road area for the money order branch and the former garage of the Registrar of Vehicles in Middle Road which was acquired and refurbished for housing the POSB operations. Further, Bala had plans drawn up in agreement with the KL Headquarters and teams of workers with an Assistant Controller in charge were sent to KL to understudy and arrange for the transfer so the relevant departments could be established in Singapore. Bertie Cheng who would eventually retire as the CEO of POSB in July 1997 was an ACP then — the youngest among the group of ACPs in Singapore. To his surprise, Bala would assign him the task of transferring the records of the POSB. Bertie Cheng recalls there were three trucks which left KL with the records and ledger cards of as many as 250,000 POSB account holders from Singapore. Till then customer details including account balances and transaction were kept in Petaling Jaya. The records were packed in crates and some even in fireproof cabinets and the loaded trucks left Petaling Jaya around 12 noon while Bertie and his staff left in cars. By then movement between KL and Singapore was already restricted and they met up with the trucks around 11 pm in Johor Baru. They returned to Singapore while the trucks spent the night in JB and proceeded with the journey afterwards.

Calamity struck when Bertie realised the next morning that two trucks had reached Singapore instead of three. But fortunately after a couple of hours of nail-biting suspense the third truck was spotted driving in to the newly acquired premises of Middle Road. Cranes had already been stationed near the office to hoist the records and equipment to the second storey but it proved to be a tricky situation. Parts of the second storey wall needed to be broken down so the larger pieces could be swung in. The unpacking continued till late into the night and though hard to believe, the team was ready for business by next morning! Eventually the Singapore POSB would be incorporated as a statutory board in 1972 and to a computerised programme which allowed it to expand.

Besides, the physical transfer, it was also felt that the postal department needed to be given a new identity and eventually postal uniforms and post box designs would be given an entirely new look. Whereas earlier the khaki-coloured uniform made of cotton required starch to stiffen before ironing, with time the current light-weight blue uniform would evolve which was far more adapted to the tropical climes. Independence also meant postage stamps needed to be directly ordered by Singapore whereas earlier they had been supplied by the KL Headquarters. So vendors needed to be sourced and fresh tenders called for. However, in the initial years till 1967, postage stamps from Malaya and Singapore were used interchangeably. But with time, stamps proved to be an excellent platform for the newly independent nation to express its own national identity and more and more time and enterprise went into the designing of the stamps. Thus on 9th August 1966, to commemorate the first anniversary of independence and as an independent member of the UPU (Universal Postal Union), the first Singapore stamps were issued. Titled, 'Survival in a Challenging Future in a Multi-racial Society', the design incorporated the three fundamentals of a young nation: Workers, Factory and Housing, and was printed by Thomas De La Rue & Co in London who used typography as the method of printing and had been printing the postage stamps since 1855. The following year the stamps issued on National Day bore a picture of a marching contingent of flag bearers and were inscribed with the legend 'Build a Vigorous Singapore' which appeared in all four official languages. Later in 1968 and 1969, on the anniversary of the National Day, the first definitive stamps of Singapore would be issued. These beautifully hand-painted stamps celebrated Singapore's multi-racial and multi-cultural society and portrayed the traditional dance forms of the three main communities, including dances as varied as the Sword Dance, the Bharatha Natyam as well as the Kuda Kepang Dance. During these first years the stamps were produced in the primary colours of red, blue and yellow, using the painstaking photogravure method of printing. With time and with the success of the first set, more definitive stamps would be issued, depicting the festivals, masks, costumes, food, art and architecture of the different ethnic groups of Singapore and the stamps would stand out as important messengers conveying not only the nation-state's diverse cultural heritage but also the importance of communal harmony which remained particularly relevant keeping in mind the racial riots of the early 1960s.[12]

Finally the transition was complete. It was a project which was well planned, well executed and completed within the envisaged timeframe. Bala's team of colleagues had served him well at a time of need and the transition was smooth. With the expanded responsibilities in Singapore and with it becoming an independent member of the UPU, as was the practice in other newly decolonised countries of the Commonwealth, the post of DOP was re-evaluated and given the title of Postmaster-General while a new position of Deputy Postmaster-General was created which was taken by Bala's dear friend and colleague, Clunies-Ross, while Rajendram headed the money order department in the new office near Orchard Road, Bertie Cheng headed POSB in Middle Road and Wong Lee Hoong headed finance. Initially, after independence the postal department would report to the Deputy Prime Minister. Later the Singapore Postal Services Department became an autonomous body under the Ministry of Communications. Subsequently, by 1982 the postal department would be merged with telecommunication and eventually by 1984 be privatised.[13]

With the difficult transition behind him, Bala soon reaped the benefits of a job well accomplished — he was surprised to find he had been nominated for the National Day Honours gold medal for public administration in the first ever National Day celebrations on 9th August 1966. While the Dutch economist and economic advisor to Singapore Albert Winsemius received the Distinguished Service Medal,

200 others from all walks of life received honours of different levels and Bala was one of them. It was a dignified ceremony at the *Istana*, the official Presidential residence of Singapore, and Bala received the medal from the hands of the first President of independent Singapore. It was a very proud moment indeed.

The same year, 1966 would be witness to yet another event that would change Bala's life forever: his marriage to Sumitra B Subramanion (née Appan). Sumitra's parents were migrants who left the shores of British India in the early 19th century for the FMS. In India they had hailed from Nagercoil in Tamil Nadu which at the time of their migration was ruled by the princely state of Travancore. Sumitra's father N A Appan was part of the Civil Service, having risen to the rank of Assistant Commissioner of Labour, Perak in 1946, like his son-in-law the first Asian to occupy such a post. Incidentally, Appan befriended the future lawyer and founding President of the Malayan Indian Congress John Thivy's family while living in Perak and the friendship would continue even when Sumitra's father moved back to India: the Thivys seeking them out during a personal visit to Nagercoil.

Sumitra was born in Ipoh in 1933 in a large family of eight siblings and her father would retire from the Malayan government service to relocate to South India in 1948. This meant Sumitra was comparatively more rooted in Indian culture than Bala, having grown up in India. She along with her siblings received a university education in India and passed out as a medical doctor. Relocating to India in 1948 when the country was still in the midst of independence fervour had its own repercussions but fortunately Sumitra was successful in gaining admission to do medicine and graduated in 1957. After completing housemanship and a three-year contract serving the Kerala government, she returned to Malaya in 1962 to comfort and support her elder sister, Bhavani Das, who was married in Ipoh and who had recently become a young widow.

And it was here that destiny took some interesting turns and she met Bala. Once in Ipoh, Sumitra joined the Malayan Medical Service and was posted in the Ipoh General Hospital, where she had been born 29 years ago. Being single she was subjected to several transfers within Perak and being unapologetically career-minded, enjoyed hospital work. However, there was constant parental pressure to marry and settle down and she met Bala quite fortuitously in KL in 1964. At that time Bala was on a holiday in KL and they would soon meet again in Singapore with their first date at the Rendezvous Hotel on Thaipusam Day!

Both Sumitra and Bala concede it did not take either of them too long to make up their minds. Despite their prolonged single status, when it was time to take a final plunge it was an easy enough decision and they married in 1966 when Sumitra was 33 and Bala 49, after a short courtship. Bala was to discover over the coming years the pleasures and pains of a domesticated life while Sumitra discovered soon enough that she had married a man who was almost inordinately devoted to his profession and besides, he was also passionate about pursuing community work in various fields. Consequently, Sumitra would have to almost singlehandedly shoulder the full responsibilities of a homemaker besides her professional duties and make a choice between hospital attachment and a clinic job which offered regular office hours. Wisely she would choose the latter.

She would also soon discover her husband's intense dislike for taking personal favours. After her marriage Sumitra applied to the Ministry of Health for a post in the government outpatient department and did not hear from them for over two months. Being a thorough professional she found the lack of a job quite frustrating. One day Dr Johnson Daniel, a close family friend, realising she was still without a job expressed his surprise that Bala was yet to put in a word with the Director of Medical Services who happened to be his close friend. With great difficulty Sumitra could convince Bala to do so and lo and behold, she was asked to join duty from the next day!

The year 1966 proved to be a singularly eventful one for Bala. The same year, the year of Singapore's first National Day celebration saw none other than Lee Kuan Yew as the Guest of Honour at the Singapore Indian Association on 9th August 1966. Bala, by then the President of SIA, had the honour of hosting him and personally escorting him around the Association's Balestier Road premises. Lee Kuan Yew would come again to SIA as a part of the third National Day celebrations while Dr Toh Chin Chye, the Deputy Prime Minister, would come for the second anniversary celebration as Lee Kuan Yew was called away for the birthday celebrations of the Sultan of Brunei.

Part of the same eventful year was also the completion of the construction work at the Sri Perumal Temple. The work which had started in 1961 and was happening sporadically because of lack of coordination, progressed rapidly after a Sub-Committee was appointed in 1964. Finally the consecration of the Perumal Temple was organised on 28th March 1966 in the presence of Minister of Social Affairs, Inche Othman Bin Wok. Despite the best efforts at fundraising by V Pakkirisamy and others, there was a shortage of funds and P Govindasamy Pillai, renowned Indian business man of Singapore who had in the 1930s founded the Indian Chamber of Commerce, generously agreed to meet the total estimated cost of more than $150,000 for the building of the marriage hall in the Perumal Temple. In recognition of his philanthropy, the hall was named after him and the first President of Singapore declared the *Mandapam* open on 19th June 1965.

The same year also saw the initiation of yet another project which would continue to be Bala's lifetime passion: the establishment of the Singapore Indian Education Trust. There was rising concern at this time about developing to the fullest the educational potentials of the Indian children so that they could effectively participate in the rapid social and economic growth of Singapore. Bala remembers the problem was unearthed in 1955 when his close friend Kandasamy was appointed Chairman of the Election Committee constituted by the PAP to contest the Legislative Assembly elections. Though Kanda discussed the issue with Bala and other friends, no corrective measures were undertaken and the problem surfaced again in 1961 when Kandasamy was Parliamentary Secretary in the Ministry of Culture. Informal discussions revealed that any educational advancement programme would require large monetary investments and with Singapore in a political turmoil nobody was willing to make such investments.

However, after Singapore's independence Kandasamy gave up his political career and instead decided to become the full-time General Secretary of the AUPE. By then he had also mustered enough social stature to be able to involve Indian professionals and businessmen in the educational project. He managed to persuade some distinguished Indians to form a pro-tem committee in 1966 and established the Singapore Indian Education Trust in 1967. A group of interested Indians would meet in August 1966 and would set up a 12 member pro-tem committee with Kandasamy as the Chairman, Bala as the Treasurer as well as significant names like K R Chandra who went on to become a Permanent Secretary in several ministries, P Govindasamy the MP, J G Advani the lawyer and K Gopalakrishnan the teacher. As a first step a draft constitution was drawn up and approved by the Registrar of Society and a scholarship fund was set up.[14]

Nurturing the Next Generation

The focus of the Singapore government remained on education. The PAP had implemented a new National Education Policy soon after it came into power in 1959 which focused on not only equal treatment of the four streams of education, viz., Malay, Chinese, Tamil and English but also on the study of Mathematics, Science and technical subjects. And this emphatic focus on education became all the more pronounced after 1965 with the PAP devoting more than one-third of its budget to education during the first nine years of its governance. With the umbilical cord with Malaysia abruptly snipped, Singapore needed to poise itself for rapid development and the citizens needed to play a vital role in this nation building process. Culturally there was need to form a forward-looking, cohesive multi-racial community and economically there was need for industrial growth to provide employment and to complement entrepôt trade. Education seemed to be the key for addressing both these concerns.

The PAP stood true to the principle of democratic socialism it had preached before independence and made meritocracy its guiding principle, i.e., an ideology which spoke of individual ability rather than race or language or social class. This proved to be a mixed blessing for the Indian community: on one hand it was a powerful beacon of hope, an opportunity to break out of any established stereotype and prove one's worth but on the other hand, it also meant a constant honing of skills and a constant need to measure up against ever-rising standards. The last proved to be a challenge, not perhaps for the top layer of the community with privileged, educated backgrounds but for the large proportion that had made humble beginnings as unskilled or semi-skilled labour or small-scale entrepreneurs in colonised Singapore. As Kandasamy commented in his National Day message of 1967, "The Singaporeans of Indian origin are less than 8% of the total population and are predominantly engaged in unskilled or semi-skilled work. A minority community is more malleable to the demagogy of a racialist, than a majority community. A minority community, which for historical reasons has been the supplier of unskilled or semi-skilled labour, is more prone to fall victim to the chauvinist, than a majority community which has a large number of members in the professional and business fields."[15] He continued by saying that many other factors could be exploited by racialists to create antagonisms between the people of different racial origins, but economic and social factors were the most vulnerable. Thus, bringing the Indian community up to mark in education, providing important professional skills were not only so they could fully participate in the social and economic growth of Singapore but also so that the future of the multi-racial nation-state was peaceful and there was no residual sense of victimisation. The purpose of SIET (Singapore Indian Education Trust) was not only to help young Singaporean Indians who seemed to have lagged behind in the government's overall educational projections and those whose performance fell below the national average but also the capable students who due to poor family circumstances were not entering institutions of higher learning.

So it was with this background in mind that the 12-member pro-tem committee formed the SIET: education was no longer an indulgence but an urgent necessity. What was more promising about the organisation for Bala was that like the Indian Association it had a pan-Indian outreach rather than being hemmed in by language, religion or dialect considerations. Bala recounts, the first issue was of raising funds for a scholarship fund. Even after a year of efforts, by 1967 the amount stood at a humble $3,297 and by 1971 at $25,000. The following year the first three official SIET scholarships were awarded. The interest from the capital sum proved to be insufficient to cover this and the committee members including Bala paid the difference of $930 from their pockets. The inaugural AGM of SIET would be held on a Sunday, 14th January 1968 at the premises of the Indian Association in Balestier Road with 126 members — six life members, of which Bala was one, and 118 ordinary ones. Bala would retire from the Management Council of the Trust only in 1998 but would continue to be associated even afterwards and eventually in 1999 the Trust Constitution would be amended under his guidance.

The year 1967 would also see Bala and Sumitra in the role of parents — their first child, a daughter Anidha would arrive, followed by their son Arjun in 1973. Sumitra reminiscences, that almost from the first day of being a father, Bala was a changed person. For her it was almost a dramatic transition as she witnessed the softer side of her husband coming to the fore. He tried to compensate for his long absences from home by spending as much time as he could on their education. As their children grew up Bala instilled in them a love for English literature. He would bring whole collections of the Lady Bird series home for them to help improve their reading skills and spend time in carefully planning their education. Anidha remembers her childhood to be a perfect balance of the east and the west. She could speak Tamil much before she could communicate in English, her father would accompany her to watch Tamil movies (though he knew little about Tamil movie stars) as much as he would accompany them for Hollywood movies and they would celebrate Deepavali and Pongal as much as they did Christmas. According to Anidha, dinner parties at home were completely British affairs, only her father and his friends would wear *veshti* while they drank their gin!

If at home Bala tried hard to achieve an east-west balance, in his community service too he remained committed to finding a balance between Indian and local influences. Thus during his tenure as President of the Singapore Indian Association, just as he hosted Lee Kuan Yew and Dr Toh Chin Chye, he also invited in October 1966 Vice President Zakir Hussain and on 19th May 1968 Prime Minister of India Mrs Indira Gandhi. On her visit the Association organised, in cooperation with other Indian organisations, a welcome gathering at the National Theatre in River Valley Road. A large number of Indians and others attended and Bala felt he was fortunate to give the welcome address. He spoke rather eloquently of the increasing necessity of Singapore and other countries in Southeast and South Asia to "play an active role in shaping not merely their national destiny but also the history and future of the whole of this region." Indira Gandhi on her part spoke to the Indian diaspora on the importance of adopting their country of migration as their own.

Even as Bala's home life and community service work were further enriched, in his professional life too he scaled new heights during this period. It was an exciting period of post-independence nation building when the tiny nation-state of Singapore was continuously on the lookout for novel avenues of growth which would help it overcome its own vulnerabilities. The POSB (Post Office Savings Bank) proved to be one of these. Right from initiation, the POSB had been run on British lines, i.e., as a small-term saving opportunity for the poor rather than in Japan where it was run more as a business model. With growth in plans of industrialisation after 1965, the Minister for Finance Dr Goh Keng Swee identified domestic savings as one of the ways to promote industrial growth. Such savings could provide the government with a non-inflationary source of funds for national development and POSB, one of the most popular low-cost banking services provided in Singapore till its gradual decline after 1955 (when the deposits had reached a level of $57 million), seemed to have great potential in this field for mobilising national savings. By 1966 the deposits were down to an all-time low of $37 million and consequently Dr Goh Keng Swee formed a Savings Bank Committee to revitalise the bank and turn around its falling deposits.

The Committee members were chosen with care from the government, business and institutes of higher learning while Bala was the Chairman and Bertie Cheng, ACP — Post Office Savings was Secretary. Its proposal of invigorating the bank was accepted by the government in July 1968 and subsequently the committee was reconstituted as an Advisory Committee to oversee the POSB's implementation of the proposal. As a part of the new plan a publicity blitz was mounted to announce the new schemes of operation of a savings account in any of the four national languages, withdrawal limits raised up to $500 and withdrawal possible once every three days. Along with this a savings competition was started among all government and government-aided schools to mobilise deposits of young account holders and an annual lucky draw was launched to attract new deposits. The lucky draw would prove to be equally popular among clients as well as television viewers and the deposits would rise steadily, reaching a figure of $42 million by 1968. The POSB would be Bertie Cheng's first responsibility after he joined Singapore postal service as a fresh graduate and he would grow with the bank as it grew from a depositor base of 250,000 in 1966 to 1 million depositors in 1976 by when it also had the rare honour of being the first local bank to go online and provide ATM service. Bertie would eventually retire as the CEO of POSB and remain a close friend to Bala.

The freshly sovereign state's need at that point was a quick mobilisation of funds, and gaming activities or public gambling proved to be yet another avenue for doing so. During the war the public amusement parks — Great World, New World and Happy World were known as the focal point of gaming while post-war the Singapore Turf Club at Bukit Timah Road was considered the only legally authorised venue for gaming. After independence, to curtail illegal operators and raise revenue, the government authorised off-the-course betting and the Turf Club was authorised to conduct the Singapore Sweep Lottery for charitable purpose. The first draw was held on 11th December 1966 with prize money of $350,000. The revenue from ticket sale was about $1.5 million and the second draw was soon held on 29th January 1967 and thereafter once every month.

Seeing the potential of revenue, in April 1968 the government announced the proposal to set up a company that would provide an avenue for legal gambling. The money realised from this would be channelized towards the benefit of citizens and for the construction of a new sports stadium in Kallang. The government announcement also indicated that a team of Bulgarian specialists would arrive to help set up the organisation as they had many years of experience in successfully operating the Bulgarian Sports Totalizator, the leader in the field of digit lottery since 1957.

Bala's involvement with the Singapore Pools began in the late 70s while he was PMG and Selvadurai Thiruchelvam, Deputy Secretary from the Ministry of Finance, discussed with him the possibility of using the GPO and other post offices for the new gaming enterprise. Eventually the Singapore Pools was established in May 1968 and Bala was one of the signatories for its incorporation along with Thiruchelvam, the eventual Chairman of the Singapore Pools, and others. In Bulgaria as well as other European countries the numbers game was called LOTO. However, in Singapore it was felt that the use of the name LOTO could be mistakenly associated with another local game of draughts, a game which is akin to the traditional chess and played on a board with 64 squares. It was therefore decided that the numbers game would be called TOTO.

The company's temporary headquarters were set up in Mountbatten Road and the recruitment of staff and sales agents was embarked upon with much enthusiasm. Eventually a staff of 230 was appointed and they were gathered in the Victoria Memorial Hall and briefed on the 6/49 game and instructed as to how TOTO coupons would be examined and accepted. The first 6/49 TOTO draw was held in the

Victoria Memorial Hall on 9th June 1968 accompanied by a musical show which was televised live. It drew a full house and the event was announced a success.

Changes and Some Fall-Outs

Bala visited Japan yet again for the 16th Universal Postal Union Congress held in Tokyo from 1st October to 14th November 1969. He realised the membership of UPU had significantly increased from 95 members in Ottawa in 1957 to 142 countries now. It was also the first time that the UPU Congress met in an Asian country and it was also the first time that Singapore participated as a sovereign country (Singapore had become a member of the UPU as an independent nation in January 1966) and Bala as PMG felt proud to represent the nation along with Lee Siow Chek, Controller of Posts.

The Congress was declared open in the presence of the Emperor and Empress of Japan by the Japanese Prime Minister at the Tokyo National Theatre. More than 800 delegates participated and nine Special Committees were set up to discuss the more than 1,000 proposals submitted by member countries. Japan had set up the first electronic voting system to expedite the work of the Congress and despite objections from Russia and East European countries, the electronic system was approved by majority vote. For the first time in UPU history translation facilities of languages other than French, UPU's only official language, were also made available. The proposals regarding letter post, air mail, insured items and parcels, finance were discussed in various meetings and Bala noticed most meetings ended on an amicable note.

There was pleasure along with work and during weekends the delegates and their wives would be taken on well-planned excursions which provided a glimpse of the age-old Japanese culture. Sumitra had accompanied Bala and greatly enjoyed the cultural shows. They also made it a point to visit Bala's old friend, Akifuji, taking a plane to Hiroshima to spend an enjoyable weekend with him and his family.

Soon the Congress came to an end: the conclusion was marked by a ceremony and the Acts of the Union were signed in the Sunflower Hall of the Tokyo Prince Hotel. The evening farewell was cordial and cheerful with participants joining in a midnight rendering of *ce n'est quún au revoir* (it is only a goodbye).

Soon after his return from the UPU Tokyo Congress, Bala decided to bid adieu to the postal service. He was 53, just a couple of years short of the compulsory age of retirement. His retirement was effective from 1st January 1971 but before that, in December 1970 he made it a point to visit all the post offices of Singapore, bidding farewell to the postmasters and their staff as well as the staff of the various departments of the GPO. On the last day, Bala recalls walking out of his office onto the balcony of the Fullerton Building and taking a last nostalgic look at the ships anchored in the bay. It had been a long journey of 34 years in the postal service and a buffet and a social gathering to commemorate retired officers was organised by the staff of the postal union on 3rd January 1971. The function was held in the St John's Ambulance Headquarters and was graced by Yong Nyuk Lin, Minister of Communication. While Bala and Clunies-Ross were the two senior officers, there were 20 other retired officers from other ranks who were commemorated as well.

Following Bala's retirement winds of change would sweep over the postal department. The *Straits Times* of 2nd April 1971 carried a report "Experts Move in for Postal Shakeup". It speaks of two experts from the National Productivity Council moving into the Fullerton Building to plan the first stage of re-organising. In continuation it also comments on the experts from NPC working in close cooperation with senior officers of the department to collect "the necessary facts and figures that will tell where [the postal department] needs to be fattened, thinned or rejuvenated." According to the report the first phase of the investigation was to last several weeks and then a new team from NPC would move in for a more detailed study. Meanwhile a group of 21 senior and middle management officers from the department had completed a special two-week course.

The history of the NPC, which in 1972, was to be taken over by a statutory body, the National Productivity Board, can be traced back to January 1965, when the National Trades Union Congress, the Singapore Manufacturers' Association and the Singapore Employers Federation signed the Charter for Industrial Progress and the Productivity Code of Practice. The intervention in the postal department was obviously a part of the nation-wide attempt to step-up productivity and modernise public services and would eventually cover not only the GPO in Fullerton but also sub and branch offices. The reorganisation study was undertaken on the recommendation of the Minister of Communication, Yong Nyuk Lin, as it was felt that the postal system, which remained a reflection of the British system, needed to be rapidly refurbished keeping in tune with the rapid changes sweeping Singapore, particularly in terms of the increased number of streets and buildings and the consequent increased number of delivery points. The article also mentions some complaints from postal workers regarding heavy peak-hour workload at public counters and some discomfort because of the heat in the sorting department located in the basement of the Fullerton Building, though they concede that the airflow and lighting systems had been improved sometime back.

This news report can be linked back to Bala's memories of Yong Nyuk Lin's visit to the GPO before his retirement. The GPO in the Fullerton Building had always been a special attraction for visiting dignitaries who would marvel at the efficiency with which postal articles were segregated, stamps cancelled as well as at the existence of the underground tunnel and the longest post office counter in the Commonwealth. However, during this particular visit Bala recalls he was faced with a bit of an embarrassing situation when the Minister was led to see how postal parcels were handled: while answering a question raised by a newspaper reporter about the air ventilation system, it was found that the ventilation system was not working that morning. Though the air was cool enough with the swirling fans and the complaint for the failure of the system had already been lodged with the PWD, Bala says the newspaper highlighted the small malfunction and he felt rather unhappy with such unpleasant publicity, particularly as the post office had generally enjoyed a good public image.

By November 1971 the *Straits Times* reports of continuing training of postal employees by the NPC both in the post offices as well as the NPC centre in Jurong. In the meantime the postal department had also put in place practices recommended by the interim report of the NPC to speedup postal delivery: there were two deliveries in most districts made possible with the recruitment of 47 more postmen, purchase of 15 scooters, 5 motorcycles with side-cars and 5 pickup vans.

But by then Bala had moved on — in October 1971 he joined Singapore Pools as a General Manager and was delighted to start work at the headquarters in Percival Road, Fort Canning Park. Earlier in the year he had relinquished the Directorship of Singapore Pools following his retirement from the civil services as PMG. He was happy to have been associated with the company since its inception and though his work with the company had been voluntary he had enjoyed every moment of it. On his retirement Singapore Pools presented him with a portable typewriter he was glad to use because by then he felt his handwriting had begun to take the shape of indecipherable ideographs! By 1971 the company was firmly established and in March 1971 the Bulgarian advisors left after the expiry of their contract. It was after this that Bala received a call from Lee Chow Soon, the Secretary of the company, who told him that even S Thiruchelvam had left on health grounds and that the new Chairman, Lim Phai Som, Permanent Secretary of Ministry of Culture, wanted to meet him as the company was considering the appointment of a new General Manager. Bala was happy to accept the offer but made it clear that the management of staff should be left in his hands without any intervention from senior officials.

By now, Singapore Pools had two weekly draws as well as periodical special draws to sustain public interest, had set up as many as 96 TOTO sales booths (though carefully placed away from schools and places of worship) and had also taken over the management of the Singapore Sweep tickets from the Turf Club with monthly draws being organised in the Kallang Park and Gay World amusement park. On joining Bala's first task was to examine the two subsidiary companies — Interad and Singapore Pools Sports Goods Co. Eventually his recommendation to wind up the latter would be accepted, while on his recommendation, Interad would continue and though revenue from advertisements secured from government or quasi-government organisations did not reach expected levels, it remained a useful arm for sales promotion.

Conclusion

The 1950s to the 1970s was one of the best periods in Bala's life. In fact during his career with the postal department he had managed to create postal history of an interesting kind. In 1858 when the Singapore Post Office was separated from the Marine Attendant's Office and became an independent department financed by postal revenue, it was one William Cuppage who became the first independent post master. In 1829 Cuppage had joined the Master Attendant's Office as a clerk and on 29th October 1858, when the Post Office became a separate department financed by postal revenues, he took over as Postmaster. Exactly 100 years later, on 19th May 1958, it was a proud Singaporean, Bala Subramanion's turn to take over the operations as Director of Posts. Not only that, Bala's retirement in 1971 also coincidentally occurred exactly 100 years after Cuppage himself went on retirement in 1871!

During the period of 1950s to the 1970s, career-wise Bala was at a zenith. But perhaps more importantly, it saw him reaching beyond the narrow, constricting walls of his own life. The transition in him was not only in terms of the community and nation building work in which he immersed himself, but also in a visible maturing of his world vision. Bala had started his life with little information of his ancestry, i.e., little in terms of an inherited past. All he grew up with was an amorphous memory of Thanjavur from where his father had migrated when a young man and of which Bala had heard from his parents, but which he perhaps treated with something of the careless indifference with which children are wont to treat the adult world.

Thereafter he had something of a straitjacketed childhood which his parents felt compelled to impose on him and his siblings to keep them safe in a strange land. Bala's first conscious personal decision in his childhood was when he discovered he was quite inordinately drawn towards English literature and actively sought out his English teacher in school for some after-school-hours discussions. He stumbled upon this pleasure of having a secret world to mull over quite by accident and it urged him for the first time to go beyond what he had been expressly told to do or prevented from doing. The fine aesthetic sensibility would remain with him and even while living under rather stringent circumstances in war-torn Singapore, he would find gratification in practicing the artistic *kanji* script. And perhaps later in his adult life, the same sensibility would be one of the triggers in his quest for a better and fuller life: the beautiful home in the tree-lined La Salle Street to which he moved in 1963 was not only a marker of success but the fulfilment of a craving for a gracious inner world.

As he grew older and was more exposed to the external world, the finer honing of his personality commenced. With each experience he evolved: if from Japanese superiors he learnt work ethics and to look at tradition and ancestry with pride, from the British he learnt a certain resilience in the face of adversity and from doctrinaire socialism the inherent justice of an equitable society. But it was in the 1960s, even as Singapore accomplished its own sovereign identity, that Bala too emerged with an evolved *weltanschauung*, a personal philosophy which encompassed religion as much as it did political convictions. And subsequently he was drawn into leadership roles of social projects, not only by dint of his considerably senior professional position, but because he was now ready to contribute: his inner growth and the consolidation of personal opinion was over and, in a way, he had found himself. After this he would of course continue to grow but the growth would be not for himself, but for others, as he learnt anew to negotiate his way so that maximum success could be achieved for the social projects about which he felt strongly convinced.

Two of his social involvements which Bala continues to be most ardent about — the Singapore Indian Association (SIA) and the Singapore Indian Education Trust (SIET) — started in this period. Both are remarkable because they are pan-Indian, looking beyond the many regional or religious divides which polarise the Indian society of Singapore. These two projects were truly in keeping with the philosophy of egalitarianism taught by Subhas Chandra Bose and the INA. Younger members of the SIA recall Bala standing at the exit point of any IA event with a bag by his side: he would hand over a SIA membership form and earnestly request for a prompt application! During his term as President of SIA from 1964–68, the most critical years when Singapore was struggling to find its own identity, he felt it was important to have a cohesive pan-Indian association with a strong voice in a multi-racial, secular society. It was an important intervention because it is during these formative years that the exact texture and quality of the future Indian voice of Singapore would be sculpted. Eventually it was also Bala and his peers who would nurture and train the current leadership of SIA.

If the SIA was an important intervention, perhaps equally so was the SIET. It helped to address an issue that was even less apparent: the large underbelly of the Indian community which was often overshadowed by the number of Indians in high-profile positions; the Indian doctors, lawyers and diplomats who seemed to steal the arch lights from the broad section of the Indian population which provided skilled and unskilled labour to Singapore and who needed to be prepared to take on the onslaught of the development programme the state was planning. Good quality education made accessible at an affordable price as well as a proactive home environment was the key if this part of the community was to break out of a cycle of negativity and missed opportunities. Bala took up this project with vigour, perhaps all the more so because he knew well the lacunas of the education system he had encountered and the privation of being pressed early into a clerical job without professional training. In his personal life too education would remain a key focus area. Sumitra remembers the careful planning he devoted to education for his children.

Two other projects which Bala was involved in during this period were the refurbishment projects for the Sri Sivan and Sri Srinivasa Perumal Temples. One wonders why this interest in religious institutes in a secular Singapore and by a not-so-overtly religious Bala, though he has always been a believer of Hinduism. Interestingly, the Hindu temples of Singapore, convenient congregation grounds for the community, became important symbols of Indian identity during these formative years. As Singapore went through the ferment of initial change and development, the temples were important cultural emblems to reinforce the existence of a minority community. The reinvigoration of the temples meant a perpetuation of the Indian voice in the panoply of voices which were clamouring for attention in multi-racial Singapore. Whether the same temples could be perceived as broadening sectarian divides in the Indian community could be delved into later. First, Indian culture, however represented at that point of time, needed to be salvaged from what was believed to be a fast engulfing cultural mainstream. Thus, the Sivan Temple, one of the older Saivite temples of Singapore was restored with the compensation amount of $50,000 received against a piece of the temple land which had been acquired by the municipality for the widening of Orchard Road. To further reinforce ties with India, craftsmen were flown in from India for the sculptural work and Indian architects were consulted. Similarly, work was undertaken for giving the Vaishnavite Perumal Temple a facelift in the 1950s. However, interestingly as a part of this restoration project, on the advice of community elders the central deity of the temple was changed from the more aggressive Narasimha (with a human torso and a lion's head and talons) to the gracious Perumal. One wonders if this decision reflected in some way the increased confidence and comfort levels of the Indian community in the now independent Singapore.

Bala's intensive involvement with social issues during this period was also perhaps the fallout of his retirement in 1971 when he left the postal service to join Singapore Pools. The latter was a smaller organisation and moreover, at the time of recruitment Bala had negotiated his terms with his superior and former colleague, Lim Phai Som, Permanent Secretary of Ministry of Culture, making it amply clear that the management of the staff should be left in Bala's hands with little intervention from the Chairman or Directors. This allowed him a certain sense of freedom and free time which he could devote to social and cultural activities. This decision to pursue his passion was perhaps in certain ways a reflection of his dear friend Kanda's earlier decision: in 1963 Kanda too had decided to give up his political office with the PAP and instead devote all his energy towards his work with the AUPE and towards trade union activities in the interest of government employees. In fact it was Kanda who persuaded Bala to join him for participation in the Hindu Endowment Board and in the founding of the Singapore Indian Education Trust.

The same period also saw Bala in the avatar of a father and a husband. Even as Singapore achieved freedom in 1965, Bala was experiencing the pleasures of a new kind of bondage: he was married to Sumitra in 1966 after a courtship of four years. The arrival of Sumitra would enrich his life in more ways than one. In her not only did he find a companion who was educated and a true contemporary, but she, who had spent a large part of her formative years in India, helped him forge new connections with his Indian roots in a way maybe his migrant parents had not managed to. Sumitra recalls Bala discovered the name of his own caste only during his marriage and subsequently in 1967, when they travelled to Southern India together, he would keep asking her questions about things he observed. They were in Sumitra's parental town of Nagercoil when senior postal officials came to visit Bala and he noticed each of them carried a lemon which they handed to him. It was Sumitra who answered his query that carrying a lemon was considered a sign of respect and he should accept gracefully. Suddenly the old incomprehensible culture of India with which he had wrestled in books and films seemed to make sense, it was as if pieces of his self were falling into place and the jigsaw was finally making sense. Sumitra reminiscences that at 49, Bala celebrated his birthday for the first time: perhaps in certain ways the celebration went beyond just a physical one but was a powerful metaphor for a celebration for a new awakening of the self!

Bala's daughter Anidha remembers him to be a loving father, strict about nothing apart from her and her brother's education. He would take pains to introduce them to the Tamil language and Indian culture. In 1957, during his first journey to India, he had had a stopover in Calcutta and there had the opportunity to watch the performance of a renowned Bharatanatyam danseuse from Madras. Years later as a father he would have Anidha admitted in the Singapore Indian Fine Arts Society (SIFAS) so she could learn the graceful Indian dance form. Sumitra recalls, he was a diligent father, perhaps at times overly so. Once when their son Arjun was sick, Sumitra had asked Bala to give him his medication every eight hours. Bala would continue to do so even after Arjun was slightly better till the boy complained of being awakened in the early hours of the morning. This was Bala's own way of ensuring the safety of his children. He had learnt early in his professional life that diligence and discipline always came with their own attending benefits and he, as a good father, was willing to walk the extra mile for his children.

Unfortunately, as he was to soon find out, the rules which could be applied with ease and success to his profession, often did not work in life. Providence was inscrutable and life came with its own set of irrational rules. His post-retirement life awaited him with its own measures of pleasure and pain.

Notes

[1] Microfilm: CD: D2014060211; CSP.64/56; Part of FC0141/14926, Malayanization Commission, File#39/4, Volume 3.

[2] Malayan Federation consisted of nine Malay States and two of the Straits Settlements and existed between 1948 and 1963.

[3] Ref: CSO.Conf.2576/54, copy#17, 30 May 1956, CM Paper # (56)4 33.

[4] This information is corroborated by *Malayanization: Statement of Policy*. Legislative Assembly, Singapore, Sessional Paper # 65 of 1956. Printed by A G Banfield, Government Printer, p. 12.

[5] *Report of the Committee on the Malayanization of the Government Service*. Printed in Government Press, Kuala Lumpur, 1954, p. 93.

[6] Ibid., pp. 112–113.

[7] *Straits Times*, 1 May 1956.

[8] Some of SIA details from founder-member R Jumabhoy's piece included in Singapore Indian Association Souvenir of 66th Anniversary Celebration, June 1989.

[9] Details of Sivan Temple from *Truth: History of the Sivan Temple*, Ed. Arun Senkuttuvan. Singapore, 1993.

[10] Singapore, Sarawak and North Borneo were federated with existing states of Malaya to form Malaysia.

[11] *Hard Truths: To Keep Singapore Going,* Lee Kuan Yew. Straits Times Press, Singapore, 2011, p. 32.

[12] Interestingly, the journey of the Singapore stamps would continue, reflecting the changing concerns and issues of the nation. Thus in 1969, a stamp series called '100,000 homes for the People' would be issued to mark the success of public housing scheme. While in 1987, the Singapore Lion Head would appear on stamps as an alternate national symbol and to commemorate '20 years of National Service' with the five partings in the lion's mane representing the ideals of democracy, peace, progress, justice and equality as embodied in the five stars of the National flag.

More interestingly, it has been recently revealed (the *Straits Times*, Singapore, 3 August 2015) that the dancing girl in the 1968 stamp which depicts an Indian dancer in a pink and green Bharatanatyam costume and was launched to promote racial harmony is actually the danseuse Mrs Santha Bhaskar of the Bhaskar Arts Academy, Singapore who had donned the costume when Bala sent a request to the Academy for a picture of an Indian dancer for use in the series of stamps titled, Masks and Dances Definitive.

[13] In 1959 when Singapore attained self-government, the postal service department was transferred to the control of the Ministry of National Development and later

to the portfolio of the Deputy Prime Minister where it remained till the merger with Malaysia. Once the merger happened in 1963, postal service became a part of a Federal Department under the Malaysian Minister of Works, Posts and Telecommunications. After independence the postal services portfolio was returned to the Deputy Prime Minister and after three years moved to report to the Ministry of Communications.

[14] Details about SIET from *A Place in the Community: SINDA at 20, Looking Back, Moving Forward,* Audrey Perera. *Singapore Indian Development Association,* Singapore, 2011; and *Singapore Indian Education Trust: The First Thirty Years, A Short History,* R O Daniel. Stamford Press, Singapore, 2002.

[15] *Singapore Indian Education Trust: The First Thirty Years, A Short History*, R O Daniel. Stamford Press, Singapore, 2002, p. 16.

Landmark Years at the Post Office

1959. Senior Civil Servants attending a course at the Political Study Centre conducted by George Gray Thomson. *Sitting. Extreme left: Bala. Fourth from left: Gerald de Cruz. Fifth from left: George Gray Thomson.*

1963–1965. Bala accompanying Yang di-Pertuan Negara Inche Yusof Ishak, first post-independence President of Singapore, viewing the sorting of letters at the GPO.

1965. Bala accompanying Tun V T Sambanthan, Minister of Communications and Works, Malaysia, viewing the Mails Branch, Sorting and Local Delivery Section in Singapore.

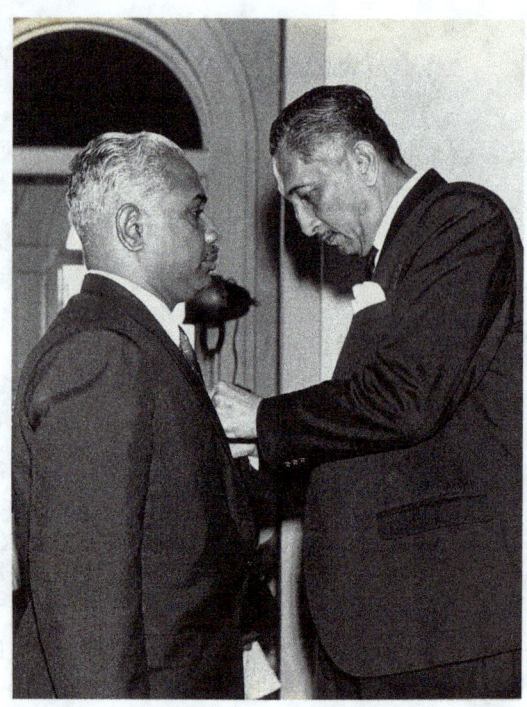

1965. Bala receiving the Public Administration Medal (Gold), known as the Pingat Pentadbiran Awam (Emas), from President Yusof Ishak at the *Istana*.

Dec 1965. Bala with Abdul Rahim Ishak, Member of Parliament for Siglap, opening the Siglap Post Office.

1968. Bala with Minister Yong Nyuk Lin to his left, examining the Stamp Cancelling machine at the GPO.

1969. Bala at the Singapore 150th Anniversary Stamp Exhibition with Koh Seow Chuan.

1970. Bala accompanying Minister Yong Nyuk Lin for presenting prizes to schools for the POSB Savings Competition.

1970. Bala presenting the Annual Award for Best Post Office, held at the GPO. *Sitting. From left: Ow Kheng Tor, Clunies-Ross, Low Siow Chek.*

Contributing to the Singapore Indian Association

Bala, President of the SIA, with committee members 1965–66. *First row. From left:* N S Menon, K T Samuel, K Gopalakrishnan, Bala, A V Devan, S R Nelson. *Second row. From left:* P Ramasamy, R Swarnam, S D Charadva, C I George, S Narayanan, Balbadhar Singh.

1966. Bala receiving Prime Minister Lee Kuan Yew at SIA for the first National Day Celebrations. With them is committee member S Thankappan.

1966. National Day Celebrations at SIA grounds. *Sitting. Front row, from left:* Mrs and Mr G Ramachandran, K T Samuel, G Kandasamy, K Gopalakrishnan, Bala's wife Sumitra, Lee Kuan Yew, Bala, Mr and Mrs A V Devan, and S R Nelson.

1966. Bala and the management committee on the occasion of a visit by the Vice President of India Zakir Hussain to SIA. *Sitting. From left:* K T Samuel, S R Nelson, K Gopalakrishnan, Mrs Alirajpur, Dr Zakir, Bala, Minister of State Haji Ya'acob bin Mohamed, Indian High Commissioner to Singapore Surendra Singh Alirajpur and A V Devan. *Standing. From left:* K P B Pillai, S Narayanan, N S Menon, C I George, S D Charadva, M B Singh, V N Rajan, M C Thomas and S Supramanian.

1968. Bala as chairman of the Welcoming Committee introducing Indira Gandhi, Prime Minister of India, to members of the Indian community at the National Theatre. *Second from left: G Ramachandran, President of the Indian Chamber of Commerce.*

1969. Visit by Mr and Mrs S Rajaratnam to SIA. *First row, from left: V N Rajan, K P B Pillai, M B Singh, A V Devan, Sumitra, S Rajaratnam, Bala and Piroska Feher, wife of S Rajaratnam.*

22nd August 2008. Visit by the 6th President of Singapore S R Nathan to SIA. *Sitting. From left: Shabbir Hassanbhai, Ambassador K Kesavapany, S R Nathan, M V Rajendran (Eddie Raj), Satpal Khattar, V P Jothi. Standing. First row, from left: Harnam Singh, Dr Kamal Bose, (unidentified), Narayana Mohan, George Dantas. Second row, from left: M Param, Bala, S Jayachandran, Vijay Iyengar, K Murali Pany.*

Involvement with the Hindu Endowments Board

Circa 1963. The Tamil actor Sivaji Ganesan's visit to the Sri Srinivasa Perumal Temple in Singapore. *Starting fifth from left: Murugian, S L Perumal, R S Sithambaram, Sivaji Ganesan, V Packirisamy, Bala.*

1965. The Yang di-Pertuan Negara of Singapore, Inche Yusof Ishak, declaring open the PGP Kalyana Mandapam (PGP Wedding Hall). *Seated. Inche Yusuf Ishak (garlanded). Seated to his left is S Rajaratnam. Bala stands behind, between the two.*

Memories of a Lifetime

1957. UPU Congress at Ottawa. *Standing. From left: Bala, Gopalakrishnan (from the Indian delegation), (unidentified), Ong Kheng Lian, Gammon.*

1966. Bala's marriage to Sumitra at the Thandayuthapani Temple in Kuala Lumpur.

1966. The couple with Dorasamy and Gouri.

1966. The couple with the Kanesans (second and third from left), who first introduced Bala to the Post Office in 1936, Bala's *amma* and close friends.

1969. UPU congress in Japan. *Starting fourth from left: Low Siow Chek, Sumitra, Bala.*

Chapter 6

We Must Make a People

Post-independence, Present Work: 1972 onwards

"But we have to work at a destiny. We stumble,
Now and then. Our nerves are sensitive.
We strive to find our history, break racial
Stubbornness, educate the mass and Educated –
Evacuate the disagreeable…
There is little choice — We must make a people."

Catering for the People, Singapore
— Edwin Thumboo

Merits of Meritocracy

The 1970s caught Singapore entering a second chapter of post-independent development. Bala too, with the same uncanny simultaneity which his life had displayed earlier with the evolution of the nation, was in the midst of a new phase of experiences. His second child and only son, Arjun was born in 1973: by now 56, Arjun's arrival further confirmed Bala's role as an experienced father and family man. He continued his employment with Singapore Pools and pursued his social work with the usual passion. His ever-growing circle of friends met regularly in the well-appointed drawing room of his home in La Salle Street and life seemed to have fallen into a beautiful and fulfilling pattern. Everything around him, like the proverbial Burmese teak or French wine, seemed to be shining better with age. Of course there was much to be achieved, but it was one of those rare moments in life when the path before him seemed clear and the destination apparent.

On the other hand, since 1965, Singapore too had carved quite a dazzling path to success. The economy had shown a pronounced upswing. Trade with Indonesia was on a rise since the end of Konfrontasi in June 1966, as was the volume of trade with Japan and the US, the latter having grown in regional presence with increasing involvement in the Vietnam War. Singapore was rapidly emerging as a financial centre and capital market: by 1968 it was the Asia Dollar Market and by 1969, a gold market, having outstripped Hong Kong and Beirut. With economic growth, infrastructural investments increased manifold as the tiny city-state of Singapore hastened to build on its strengths and shore up against its weaknesses. Always known as a port city, it offered tax-free registration to foreign ships and expanded its shipping lines and soon was the busiest port in the Commonwealth and by 1975, the largest port of the world, after Rotterdam and New York. In 1975 the last British naval units and helicopters too left and by March 1976, British withdrawal from Singapore was complete. Though initially, when plans of withdrawal of British security forces were announced there was some insecurity given the island's position, surrounded by hostile nations, a solution was devised to this problem too: under soon-to-be Deputy Prime Minister, Dr Goh Keng Swee's advice, Singapore decided to build a small regular army supported by a large force of national servicemen, a result of a policy of universal male conscription.

In the meantime the island's skyline was fast changing with large scale drainage schemes, projects on urban renewal and finally the homeownership scheme under the Housing and Development Board. The direct fall out of such urban renewal was a dramatic rise in health standards — life suddenly had more to offer than tuberculosis and early death. But even as decaying squatter colonies gave way to modern cost-efficient high-rises, much of the old, semi-rural way of life and the warm sense community living that Bala had known, seemed to disappear. Singapore was proudly marking its place in a new-age Asia.

So what did this mean for the Indian community? Even as Singapore bravely made its way through the glut of physical and infrastructural issues which have traditionally held Asia down? Turnbull points out that Socialism, the platform on which the PAP had initially courted the Singapore electorate, was one of the first casualties. There was need to shed doctrinaire Socialism if "nervous foreign capital" and "reluctant local capitalists" were to be reassured and channelised.[1] This, along with a decision to avoid the concept of a welfare state based on the Western model, meant Singapore would focus on policies which 'enabled' the citizenry rather than provided and subsidised for them. This again meant a focus on a good education and opportunities for skill building or in other words, a policy of meritocracy by which each individual would have the opportunity to enhance his life through skill and effort. For the freshly independent nation with a blossoming confidence in its economic prowess, meritocracy seemed to be an ideal solution in more senses than one. It brought with itself an attendant environment of human endeavour and discipline which bred solidarity in a multi-cultural society while this new sense of nationhood injected fresh energy into the system and an enduring will to survive.

A glance at the activities undertaken by the Singapore Indian Association (SIA) during this period is a clear indication of how the new culture of Singapore impacted the Indian community, how it was assimilated and what steps were taken in response.[2] Firstly, there was renewed emphasis on sports. Though Bala by the 1970s was no longer the President of SIA, his close association with the Association continued and he being a keen sportsman himself was one of the forerunners in driving the sport initiatives. In the early 70s several sportsmen like H S Dhillon for hockey and Hussein Shah for cricket became members of the Management Committee and the association could produce many talented sportsmen.[3] This was a period when SIA for the first time won various championships at home and also had the first tour organised for participation in the prestigious Murugappah Gold Cup Hockey Tournament of Madras. The SIA's hockey team would emerge as national champions in Singapore and this association with competitive sports activities would continue in the future too. The advantages of such sports activities were many — they were clearly a way to provide the Indian community with a cutting edge advantage over others in a nation given to a policy of universal conscription and where the formation of national level sports teams was still at a nascent stage. It was also an opportunity to build on inherent strengths of the community and provide discernible avenues of growth for the Indian youth in a career sufficiently disassociated from the role an Indian was traditionally expected to play in Singapore — that of a skilled or unskilled labour. Sports added a welcome new dimension to the stereotype.

Bala as the President of SIA, had the honour of hosting and personally escorting Lee Kuan Yew around the premises of the association for Singapore's first National Day celebrations on 9th August 1966. As the Guest of Honour what the Prime Minister mentioned was significant. Making a clear reference to the "desire for ascendancy" in a plural society he reminded the Indians that they were "in a different milieu which requires different attitude and adjustments."[4] In his typical candid way, it was a gauntlet he had thrown in the arena. It was up to the community as to how they would respond.

Of course as a direct response to this the SIET (Singapore Indian Education Trust, discussed in earlier chapter) was formed, the brainchild of G Kandasamy, which during the formative years shared the premises of SIA and in which Bala too played a key role. But along with this other steps were undertaken as well to further enrich and enable the community.

Thus the Academy of Fine Arts with a new board of governors was established in 1971. The SIFAS or the Singapore Indian Fine Arts Society was one of the earliest cultural organisations, established in 1949 after the return of the British at the end of Second World War. But though there had been an initial increase in student membership, the society had continued to be beset by financial problems. Besides, the Management Committee members found it difficult to administer the teaching programme as well as undertake public performances. But now there was renewed focus on the society as not only a way to promote the Indian fine arts including dance and music but as a means of helping the new generation Indians to stay in touch with their cultural roots. Perhaps it was felt that such cultural integration with their past was necessary to bolster the migrant community's confidence in what was emerging to be the increasingly challenging environment of Singapore.

In 1973 the Society moved from its own premises in St Michael Road to a two year rent-free accommodation in Branksome Road, made possible by the generosity of one R Balasubramaniam. Subsequently, in 1982 it would move to the vacated Rumah Miskin Police Station in Balestier Road and finally in the early 1990s to its present premises in Starlight Road, off Serangoon Road. Bala became a member of SIFAS in 1972 at the request of one Mr Narasimhan who was active in the building fund committees of the Perumal and Sivan Temples. But Bala's interest would be triggered only after his daughter, Anidha was enrolled there as a dance student. This was in Branksome Road when he agreed to be on the board of governors and was entrusted with the dance portfolio of the unique Indian dance form of Bharatanatyam. In fact in this Bala was persuaded by the late Dr V S Rajan, the then head of Middle Road Hospital, who was actively involved in the reorganisation and development of SIFAS.

It perhaps does not need to be mentioned that Bala, so far in his life had had little exposure to dance! Apart from some tricks of ballroom dancing which he had picked up while in the UK, this was yet again another *tabula rasa* which life threw at him. As was his usual practice, he decided to start at the basic: as a first step he decided to learn something about the dance form: Sumitra recalls the books on Bharatanatyam that he pored over during this time (SIFAS conducted classes in Carnatic music, veena, mridangam, violin and the dance forms of Bharatanatyam and Kathak). Finally, a syllabus of study was finalised for the dance academy with the help of three eminent professionals — Professor S Sambamoorthy, Dr S Sita and S Balachander, and a weekly timetable was drawn up. Teachers were instructed to adhere to the schedule and follow the prescribed syllabus. Closer supervision of the classes being undertaken elicited some shortcomings: Bala and his colleagues realised that the musical scores of the *veena* course were manually written by the teacher and then copied down by the students. Not only was the process time consuming but it also had plenty of chances of error. Bala with his friend from the Tamil Division of the Radio Broadcasting Station, Murugayan, decided to enlist the assistance of the renowned maestro Pandit Ramalingam, and together they had the musical notes written and then cyclostyled. Initially the *veena* teacher Padmavathy was uncooperative and refused to teach by the prepared scores but towards the end of the term, she voluntarily came forward to write a book for the use of the first year music students. Thus the book called *Shadjam* was published in 1982 and subsequently a second book *Rishabham* and later a more comprehensive and well researched third book was published. The publication of these three books with financial assistance from the National Arts Council, Singapore was a singular achievement for SIFAS and a long journey which Bala and his colleagues had traversed since 1973 and the first aborted project.

During this time, as yet another step towards scaffolding the Indian community against the upsurge of meritocracy, the Education Sub-committee of the Hindu Endowment Board (HEB) was established. Though his involvement with HEB went back to the time when he as Director of Posts, it was in 1973 that he was appointed the Chairman of the Education Sub-committee, meant for promotion of education among the Hindu youth and for a better understanding of Hinduism in the community. The first task of the Sub-committee was to undertake an in-depth study of the lacunas in understanding and then design a programme of activities in response. It was felt that the community needed a more holistic understanding of the Vedantic roots of the religion and to clearly differentiate this from the ritualistic practices that the faith had devolved into. It was decided that local as well as Indian religious speakers would be invited and regular lecture classes would be conducted though it was also agreed that the temples would be actively encouraged to prepare their own programme of educational activities. But unfortunately, though the Education Sub-committee remained active during the initial years, public response was not encouraging. Though S Dheivanayagam did ensure Sunday classes were conducted at the Perumal Temple from 1977 to 1979, soon it was increasingly difficult to find spiritual teachers. Along with this there was the problem of finding accommodation for the teacher in the temple premises.

Subsequently, at a meeting in April 1981 the Education Sub-committee met to review its work since its incorporation in 1973. The members were unanimous in their agreement that substantial amount of work needed to be done in teaching the true tenets of Hinduism and that the Hindu temples of Singapore could play a crucial role in this area. The Committee thereafter decided to resign en bloc to provide the HEB with an opportunity to establish a new committee to plan for the tasks ahead. As the Chairman, it was Bala who submitted the letter of resignation on behalf of the committee. But unfortunately, subsequently no response from the HEB was received to acknowledge the dissolution of the Education Sub-committee or for a new appointment and it remains Bala's lasting regret that the temples have made little progress in teaching Hinduism to their parishioners and what he perceives as little active involvement in social welfare activities. He continues to firmly belief that keeping the complexity of the religion in mind, there needs to be teaching sessions on Hinduism conducted by scholars in formalised classes rather than it merely happening in the home environment.

Yet another of Bala's forays into social work during this period was being appointed as a member of the Rent Conciliation Board in November 1973 along with Yeo Joo Lim, Mohammed bin Haji Ali and Ngui Kiat Chuan. The Control of Rent Ordinance had been passed at the end of the war by the returning British colonial administration to prevent any unreasonable increase of rents by landlords during the post-war period when there was an extreme shortage of rented accommodation. It was in this connection that the Rent Conciliation Board was established to hear petitions from tenants for the fixing of rents of rent controlled premises as well as appeals by tenants for repair of premises or by landlords when tenants sublet the premises or when they apply for reimbursement when road widening was initiated by the government. Though Bala enjoyed this voluntary work, in 1997 the Singapore government would announce that rent control would be lifted eventually by 2001 as the number of rent-controlled premises had reduced to a meagre 1600 from some 7600 in 1989 and the Rent Conciliation Board was hearing fewer and fewer appeals. The Rent Control Act would be finally repealed in 2001 and Bala would soon receive a letter from F E R Remedios, Chairman of the Rent Conciliation Board, ending his participation of 28 years in the board. Though subsequently there would be some popular discontent that attainment of a first world status or the existence of a responsive public housing programme did not justify the abolition of such an act, the government would eventually repeal the law.

In a similar experience of public service, Bala would have the opportunity to serve on the Income Tax Board of Review. The Board, constituted under the Income Tax Act of Singapore and consisting of no more than 30 members appointed by the Ministry of Finance, was meant for hearing appeals from dissatisfied tax payers with the assessments raised by the Commissioner of Inland Revenue. The members were to hold office for a term of three years but were eligible for reappointment while the Chair of the Board was required to be a qualified District Judge. The Board was invested with considerable powers, functioning as a District Court in the context of enforcement of attendance of witnesses, hearing evidence on oath and punishment for contempt.[5] Bala was invited to serve as a board member first in August 1976 while Justice T S Sinnadurai was Chairman of the Board and subsequently was reappointed in 1979 and 1982. The appointment did not involve too much of work because cases were spread over the 30 odd members. His nine years of engagement with the Board would end in 1985.

Working with the Tamil Community

The Tamils Representative Council (TRC) was formed in 1951 with a primary purpose of bringing together the various Tamil organisations of Singapore and to serve the cultural and social needs of the community. Though the Council had continued, it was in quite a moribund state by 1978 when G Kandasamy, Bala's friend and Secretary of the AUPE was brought in for its revival.

Bala's association with the TRC started the same year with a personal invitation from Kandasamy to attend a seminar organised by the Council in November 1978. He was informed that the meeting was being held with the objective of discussing the problems faced by the Tamil community in educating their children and raising their skills to participate fully in the success story of Singapore. During the course of discussion, as one paper after the other was read out, it became increasingly evident that there was rising concern amongst Tamil parents that the facilities offered by Singapore schools for teaching Tamil were often not adequate or encouraging and there was a rising trend of Tamil children opting to study Malay or Chinese as their second language.

What was apparent to Kanda, Bala and their colleagues at the TRC seminar was of course the tip of the iceberg. The background, as they were to discover, went far deeper and spanned several years of history. For several years now academic success in Singapore had been defined by not only success in the core subjects but also the ability to do reasonably well in the languages (Malay, Chinese or Tamil). The bilingual education policy which was configured on the study of the English language plus a mother tongue was originally premised on the expectation that nearly everyone could be effectively bilingual.[6] But as the years passed the inherent difficulties of such a policy became apparent: not all children could pick up two languages at the same level. And then came the then Deputy Prime Minister Dr Goh Keng Swee's Report on Education which was to be implemented from 1979 onwards. According to the report, students according to their academic results were first to be streamed at nine years of age (Primary 3) into the Extended (EM1), Normal (EM2) and Monolingual (EM3) streams with the latter being the weakest group of students who were not required to study their mother tongue. Subsequently, between 1991 and 2004, streaming would be conducted at 10 years of age, i.e., in Primary 4.

Now, one wonders what the reason for concern was in the Indian community about what appeared to be a fair scheme. Was it that the Indian children were being streamed either in EM2 or EM3 categories for their poor academic results? Perhaps that, but how did that reflect on the study of the Tamil language? The answer to that question lay in the minority status of the Tamil community. The fact cannot be denied that despite Malay, Mandarin, Tamil and English being adopted as the four official languages of Singapore, it was Tamil which was the only language which did not enjoy any privileged position or serve any apparently pragmatic purpose. The Malay language written in a Roman script, though spoken by a small section of the population, had the unique position of being the sole national language and as such is a symbolic political gesture towards recognising the geopolitical realities of Singapore. Chinese, on the other hand was the language spoken by the ethnic majority and moreover it was a language which received considerable boost from the government for trade and business reasons. English of course had since colonial times been the language of commerce and government and the virtual *lingua franca* for Singapore. In contrast was Tamil spoken by a thin sliver of the multiracial community and in the study of which many of the Tamils themselves saw little future prospect. The smallness of the Tamil medium is apparent in a comment by Lee Kuan Yew himself, "On 8 December 1959, I made my first major speech on the importance of having a bilingual education system. It was at the Gay World Stadium, the biggest covered stadium in Singapore. There were 10,000 teachers and principals in the audience. I told them of the 320,000 students in their charge: 51% in English-medium schools, 43.5% in Chinese, 5% in Malay and 0.5% in Tamil."[7]

To break down racial barriers the PAP would introduce a concept of Integrated Schools in 1960 where teachers and students from two or more schools of different language streams were brought together under one administration. In such Integrated Schools in the morning the classes could be in English while in the afternoon, they could be in Chinese, Malay or Tamil, depending on which schools came together. The first such school would be the Bukit Panjang Government High School and by 1968, one in six primary and secondary schools was a part of the Integrated Schools programme. Though the programme would be abandoned subsequently, it is a useful example to illustrate the problems which were highlighted at the TRC Seminar of 1978: because of the miniscule status of the Tamil medium the number of Tamil schools which could participate in such programmes would remain at a minimum, thus further inconveniencing parents who were keen to have their children study Tamil. Besides, after 1966 it was no longer a matter of choice. Study of Tamil became compulsory for children with Tamil-speaking fathers as the Education Ministry laid down a definitive description of mother tongue as, "the symbolic language of the group of one's paternal ancestry, rather than the language of one's primary socialization, or one's native speech."[8] And then in 1969 second language became a compulsory examination paper in the GCE O-levels, in 1973 it was decided that double weighting would be attached to second language in the Primary School Leaving Exams (PSLE), giving it an emphasis equal to the first language, and finally in 1979 came Dr Goh Keng Swee's report on streaming.[9]

It was against this background that the TRC Seminar took place and eventually the report on mother tongue education would bring new emphasis and a strong impetus in the study of Tamil and simultaneously bring to light the serious systemic lacunas. The TRC would undertake a detailed scrutiny of the facilities available for the study of Tamil in schools and find several areas which required early attention. Representations would be made to the Ministry of Education and Bala and his colleagues would have a fruitful discussion with then Senior Minister for Education and current President of Singapore, Dr Tony Tan. The highlights of the discussion would cover the following:

- Good government and some of the aided missionary schools often did not offer Tamil
- There was need for Tamil to be taught in all primary and secondary schools as well as junior colleges
- There was need to introduce Tamil literature as a part of the A-level examinations
- There was need to train Tamil teachers to be alternatively bilingual, so that they could conduct other language classes as well

Almost simultaneously the TRC launched a vigorous campaign to enlighten and encourage Indian parents to have their children enrolled for Tamil as their second language. Keeping the Prime Minister's view in mind on *cultural ballast*, i.e., his belief that language transmits values, the TRC too emphasised the traditional values which were inherent in the study of Tamil literature, particularly of the ancient Tamil Sangam literature and the *Tirukkural*. However, the TRC realising that Tamil students needed to be proficient in other subjects as well besides their mother tongue if they were to emerge successful in the streaming system, sought to start a tutorial programme wherein private tuitions would be made accessible for disadvantaged families. In 1979, with this sole purpose the TRC Educational Assistance Programme (TRC–EAP) was launched and tutorial classes commenced at the Ramakrishna Mission of Norris Road and at the Siglap Community Centre. However, the initial enthusiasm soon wore off as they faced difficulties in recruiting volunteer teachers to participate in the experimental project.

However, the project received a boost when in 1982 a pilot scheme was started for 107 Primary 6 students at the Umar Pulavar Tamil High School. Classes were conducted in all subjects for 10 continuous Sundays and eventually this time the project was declared a success. It was a brainchild of the renowned scholar Dr A Veeramani, lecturer at the National University of Singapore, who as advisor to the TRC–EAP had worked out not only an excellent tuition scheme but also prepared a detailed manual for its implementation, and with his characteristic charisma had even enlisted the help of 10 volunteer teachers!

Encouraged by positive results the TRC–EAP scheme was expanded gradually in the following years to include students from Primary 3 to 6 and some classes of the Secondary school as well. Unfortunately, Dr Veeramani would eventually leave TRC but the TRC Education Committee with Bala as Chairman would continue and with the active participation of compatriots like K Illangovan (General Secretary), P Chandran (Treasurer) and V K Gopal, the TRC–EAP scheme would eventually be rolled out for as many as 2,624 students and 249 volunteers with classes to be conducted in 13 schools.

Bala recalls an interesting anecdote from this period. When the TRC–EAP initially started the classes in Umar Pulavar Tamil High School they were discouraged to note the lack of student engagement. The children seemed to remain dispirited and inattentive despite the best efforts of the teachers. It was then that they realised that many of the children who came from less privileged backgrounds were actually attending the Sunday morning classes without having eaten breakfast. Local Indian vendors of the Serangoon Road vicinity (the Umar Pulavar Tamil High School is in Beatty Road) came to their assistance: small packets of free food were distributed among the students before they began lessons and after that Tamil grammar and algebra were digested with ease!

In fact, one of the main problems for the EAP remained finance. The students were charged a nominal sum of $8 per subject for a term of 10 Sundays with students from needy homes being exempted from it. There was difficulty in organising donations too as the programme continued for multiple years and the fund sources were soon drying up. Eventually, the TRC would decide to start a GIRO donation appeal and launch a mass campaign for a small contribution of $5 or more in July 1987.

Fortified by the financial support received from the GIRO donation fund, the TRC was able to continue its yearly EAP successfully. By 1990 the programme stabilised with a yearly intake of around 2,000 students in 10 school centres spread through the island. It was a well-conceived plan which had been well executed and justifiably made Bala both happy and proud. He had become a member of the TRC in 1978 and was appointed Chairman of the Education Committee, entrusted with the management of the TRC–EAP in 1982. Later, on Kandasamy's persuasion he accepted the appointment of Vice President — Education to facilitate communication with ministries as well as quasi-government bodies. In 1990 he would hand over the education portfolio to Amoganathan, an educationist and principal of a secondary school. Subsequently, Bala would be elected Vice President — Publicity and eventually after two years in the position would decide not to accept any further appointment and instead retire from the field of TRC activities.

But while he was with the TRC, Bala had the proud privilege to work on the preparation of two crucial reports: the first being TRC's *Submission on Core Values and National Ideology* made in September 1989 to the present day Prime Minister of Singapore, Lee Hsien Loong, who was then the Minister for Trade & Industry, Second Minister for Defence as well as Chairman of National Ideology Committee, and the second being the report of the TRC's *Indian Children Educational Task*

Force in August 1989 made to S Chandra Das, Member of Parliament and Advisor to TRC.

The first report was prepared by a study group comprising Dr C R Marthandan, Dr S Gopinathan, S Muthiah, N Subramanian, S Dheivanagayam and Bala himself. It dealt with the contributions the Tamil community could make in the formulation of a National Ideology and Core Values to be adopted by all Singaporeans. The report not only outlined basic Core Values but also recommended a programme of implementation in schools as well as delineated the role of the media and cultural organisations. The background to the issue about the Core Values yet again lay in one of Goh Chok Tong's addresses. While speaking to the PAP Youth Wing in October 1988 he proposed the creation of an official "national ideology" comprising a set of shared values to anchor Singapore society and protect it from an encroaching Western influence.[10] During his opening address to the seventh parliament on 9th January 1989, then President Wee Kim Wee reiterated the same need. Subsequently, a committee led by Minister Lee Hsien Loong was convened to identify and set the government's position on the shared values, and to ensure that the values would be common across different communities, feedback was solicited from different ethnic and religious groups. It was in this context that the TRC was involved in the preparation of such a report.

What is interesting about the report is the way it cites Tamil Sangam literature to find close parallels between the Core Values suggested by the government and moral values taught by the *Tirukkural*, the book of couplets or *kurals*.[11] For the dissemination of such Core Values the report suggested schools be used as a vehicle and moral science be included not only as a separate subject but the same values be inculcated through a suitable rendering of historical stories and literary illustrations. Indeed moral and citizenship education would be a part of the school syllabus of Singapore though such education would be divested of any religious connotations and instead focus on certain values which were considered important to achieve social cohesion.

The second report from the TRC was submitted by the *Indian Children Educational Task Force (ICETAF)*, which had been established by the TRC in 1987 and consisted of a wider selection of members from the Indian community. The ICETAF had been established because a Tamil Youth Seminar organised by the TRC once again highlighted the problem of the falling academic attainment of Indian students: there was still an over-representation of Indians in the monolingual stream (EM3) of the Primary and the normal stream (EM2) of the Secondary schools, poor performance in English, Maths and Science had also continued, and at university level Indians naturally gravitated towards the Arts and Social Sciences rather than Engineering or Science courses. Though intermittent efforts had been made to improve the situation by certain organisations, at this point the TRC felt that it called for a more well-coordinated drive and thus the ICETAF was formed comprising Indian principals of Primary and Secondary schools and experienced educationists. The report suggested a more holistic approach rather than just providing tutorial classes. Instead it was felt the home environment also played a role in the students' performance and so parents were also to be included under a single umbrella programme and encouraged to provide a more conducive environment for study. One of the key recommendations was the setting of a National Committee for the Educational Advancement of Indian Children (NCEAIC), headed by a Member of Parliament or a senior respected member from the Indian community and invested with the required authority to plan, organise and implement a system of coordinated action to enhance the educational achievement of Indian students.

The report and the suggested action plan was far more detailed this time than the TRC–EAP which had been launched in 1979 and it was this enhanced plan of 1989 which would be the precursor to the establishment of SINDA (Singapore Indian Development Association) in August 1991 and the appointment of the Action Committee on Indian Education by Indian Members of Parliament in June 1991. Besides, the TRC–EAP, yet another forerunner to SINDA was the

Career Enhancing Unit started by the Singapore Indian Education Trust (SIET) in collaboration with TRC in 1989. With enthusiastic guidance from educationists like S Chandra Das, President SIET, questionnaires were sent for feedback from graduate students and gradually an information data bank was built up. However, the formation of SINDA as a central organisation for the coordination of Indian social, cultural and educational bodies had already been announced and the Career Enhancing Unit would disband itself since it felt its own activities should more properly come under the aegis of SINDA.[12]

Bala played an integral role in the ICETAF and subsequently would continue to do so in SINDA. He would present a paper on the TRC's Educational Advancement Programme (Achievements and Challenges) at the 6th Seminar on Tamil Language and Tamil Society in Singapore organised by the National University of Singapore Tamil Language Society on 18th July 1987 and in 1988 and 1989 have the honour of welcoming the guests of honour (K Shanmugam, MP for Sembawang GRC in 1988 and present Home Affairs Minister and J Y Pillay, Managing Director, Monetary Authority of Singapore in 1989) as well as speak about the TRC's educational interventions at the annual Awards Day of the TRC–EAP.

Even as Bala focused on his community work, his employment with the Singapore Pools had continued. In fact when he joined as General Manager, TOTO sales were not progressing well and therefore various measures had been adopted. The prize structure had been altered to enhance its popularity, a new variation of the game called ABC TOTO was introduced (though withdrawn in 21 weeks) and the jackpot had been increased by $5,000 for every draw until it was won. Not surprisingly these changes attracted almost double the number of bets for each draw in 1981. Finally the 1 million dollar prize was introduced in 1982 with an issue of 2.6 million tickets at $2 each and this too proved to be a grand success. By 1983 the sales turnover had risen to about $87 million, a singular achievement considering unlike in Canada or Australia, radio and television publicity for gaming was not allowed in Singapore (discontinued by the Broadcasting Department in December 1978). With the steady growth it was felt that certain sections of the Singapore Pools needed to be computerised and Bala enlisted the help of his old colleague Bertie Cheng who was by then with the POSB Bank. The management of the Sweep lottery section was first to be computerised, followed by the Payroll and Accounts.

Bala recalls the interesting beginning of having the TOTO games computerised. It was he who came across by chance an article in a magazine about a numbers game LOTO operated by portable machines in Canada. It was reported that the machines were easy to operate, the game itself was popular and the revenue so raised was used for the welfare of the people. It was subsequently that the Singapore Pools established contact with GTECH, the suppliers of the machines. Apparently the states of South Australia had accepted GTECH's proposal for the use of GTECH soft and hardware in managing the 6/49 LOTO game. Subsequently, in 1969, Bala and the Secretary, Lee Chow Soon visited Adelaide for an overview of GTECH's operating system and what they saw was subsequently taken into consideration when changes were introduced to the Singapore TOTO game. Soon after their visit, Guy Snowden of GTECH visited Singapore and extended an invitation to Singapore Pools to send representatives to look at the operations of their machines in Canada.

Singapore Pools however decided to have yet another look at the LOTO games in Australia, a country closer home. It was later in 1982 that a team headed by the Chairman Wong Lee Hoong went to Canada. Bala and his colleagues in the team had discussions with the President of the Ontario Lottery Corporation in Toronto and had the opportunity of looking into GTECH systems operating in Toronto and Quebec. They also travelled to the US for discussions with the New York State Lottery (Albany), General Instrument (NY), GTECH (Rhode Island) as well as other gaming equipment suppliers. In 1983 Singapore Pools decided to go online and eventually would award the online project to an American supplier to GTECH along with its Singapore partner, Singapore Computer Systems in early 1985.

Since Bala joined in 1971 there had been changes in the chairmanship. First Lim Phai Som was succeeded by Lee Keng Tuan in 1974 and on his retirement in 1976, in an interesting coincidence, Bala's former postal colleague Wong Lee Hoong from the Ministry of Communication who had been a member of the board, was appointed Chairman. However, such a reversal of the official hierarchy did not affect their personal relationship, with Wong Lee Hoong insisting that Bala continue to call him by his first name. This proved to be a period of significant change and Wong Lee Hoong would ably lead the company towards enhanced efficiency, finalise the contract with GTECH and pave the way to the introduction of the fascinating Timeline TOTO Game in Singapore.

Bala bid farewell to Singapore Pools in October 1985 after a fruitful 14 years. Like in the postal department, here too he had managed to maintain cordial terms with young and old alike and even with the trade union leaders when the union was formed. His farewell party in 1985 would be personally attended by trade union members as well as the NTUC representative, William Tan. In fact, for Bala the time spent with the Singapore Pools was one of the most cherished periods of his life, a period he fondly recalls even today when he meets his former Secretary, Mary Ow, and the Staff Manager, Janice Lee.

Yet Other New Beginnings

The issue of minority representation in the Singapore Parliament was first raised in July 1982 by Prime Minister Lee Kuan Yew and it was subsequently in 1988 that the concept of GRCs or Group Representative Constituencies came into effect following amendments to the Constitution of the Republic of Singapore and the Parliamentary Elections Act in 1988. The GRC was an electoral division or constituency represented by a team of multiracial candidates and was introduced with the purpose of ensuring a multiracial parliament in the future. The GRC scheme was first introduced in the 1988 General Elections and as a corollary to this the Parliamentary Elections Indian and Other Minority Committee was established. It was stipulated that candidates were to obtain a certification from either the Malay Community Committee or the Indian and Other Minority Committee to be found eligible for candidacy in the 1988 elections.

Bala was appointed by the then President of Singapore Wee Kim Wee as a member of the Parliamentary Elections Indian and Other Minority Committee in 1988, along with other stalwarts like the Chairman K R Chandra (Permanent Secretary in several ministries), Dr Vijiaratnam (Chairman of the Tamil Murasu Board), Brigadier (Retd) Kirpa Ram Vij and Rudolph William Mosbergen. They were entrusted with the task of scrutinising the candidate applications which the committee received and Bala found it gave him a rare opportunity to know in advance those who would be contesting the elections and from which constituency! It was a rare honour and it was bestowed on Bala yet again when he was appointed a member of the Committee for the next Parliamentary Elections of 1991. In fact, despite reservations expressed by many, including his close friend Kandasamy, right from the beginning Bala has been supportive of the PAP government's move to introduce the GRC system in 1991. He recollects S Chandra Das (Chong Boon MP) discussing the issue with the Tamil Representative Council when the scheme was yet to be launched. As TRC's President, Kanda agreed to go along with the idea after some reluctance since it was felt the scheme would make it difficult to find suitable minority candidates and there would be difficulties in making cash deposits for such a candidate. The subsequent day, K Illangovan (General Secretary — TRC) faxed a handwritten TRC acceptance to Das that received much publicity. Soon the government launched a campaign for the people to sign the Great Pledge Book. Bala was one of those who accompanied Kanda when he went to sign the Pledge Book along with other TRC members.[13]

Yet another new beginning of this period would be Bala's association with the newly established umbrella body for education of the Indian community, SINDA, in 1991. But along with this association his earlier work with organisations like the SIET (Singapore Indian Education

Trust) would also continue. The fund raising efforts of the SIET were continued and by end of year 1996 the trust funds exceeded $1.7 million and in 1997 it was able to provide scholarships and awards amounting to more than $155,000 made available to 561 students. After 30 years of active participation Bala decided to retire in 1998 and yet continued in a supportive role, and in 1999 took on the task along with R O Daniel, the then Internal Auditor of SIET, of revising the SIET Constitution and incorporating the amendments which had been initiated since its inception. Further he was also able to persuade Daniel to write a short historical account of the SIET. The result of this was a booklet entitled, *Singapore Indian Education Trust: The First Thirty Years*, published with financial support of Dr R Theyvendran and presented to SIET members during the function marking SIET's 35th Anniversary on 9th November 2002. Regrettably, Daniel passed away unexpectedly on 23rd April 2003 though he left behind valuable legacy and at the SIET AGM of May 2003 it was decided that a trust fund in the memory of Roy Oliver Daniel would be established for his contributions.

Bala's active participation with SIFAS (Singapore Indian Fine Arts Society) also continued on an equal footing. He recounts wonderful years of closely working with N Subramanian, partner with Earnst & Young, Singapore and Chairman of the Board of Governors of SIFAS who he believes set the Society on its progressive march. It was under his Chairmanship that the Society was able to revise the music and dance syllabus, introduce a yearly calendar, rationalise the employments terms and conditions of the teachers and revise the tuition fees structure. They worked closely in the revision and reprinting of the Society's Constitution and it was N Subramanian who supported the Society's move to the new premises in Starlight Road with enthusiastic fund raising drive as well as with personal donations. The Board of SIFAS was dissolved in 1989 but Bala, as member of the Academic Committee, continued to be in charge of the dance portfolio. However, it was in December 1997 that, keeping in mind his advancing years, Bala declined to continue with the appointment and on 28th August 1999 the Vice President of SIFAS A Sachithananthan conferred on him the Long Service Award Gold Medal for dedicated efforts to the Society. But Bala, even after retirement remained a Trustee, thus continuing his association with the Indian arts in Singapore.

Besides, N Subramanian, Bala recalls I S Menon as one who made remarkable contributions to the development of the SIFAS. Mr Menon was employed at the Shaw Brothers when he took over the position of General Secretary in 1971. Despite the voluntary nature of the work he would come over to the society directly after office and stay on up to 9pm, turning up regularly on Saturdays, Sundays and holidays as well. He continued with the society even after retirement, diligently handling the increasing administrative work load. In 1986 he was appointed Executive Secretary, a post he executed till 1992. In memory of his contribution, after his demise in 2000 an I S Menon Memorial Scholarship Fund was established with SIET.

Amidst all his associations with social organisations, Bala's memories of the SIA (Singapore Indian Association) remain one of the most cherished. On 17th July 1989 the then President of SIA, Leslie Netto, conferred on him an honorary membership in memory of his leadership during the crucial years of 1964 to 1968 and his contributions in the field of education. Bala in turn continues to untiringly seek out new members of the Indian community and ensure their membership with the SIA — a fact that has found special mention in the memorandum of the SIA's Annual General Meeting of 16th March 2008. He notes with pride that the SIA presently stands as a 'premier centre for the promotion of sports and other social activities for the Indian community' and acknowledges the excellent work done by current President K Kesavapany and other committee members in the revival of the SIA and the large-scale refurbishment of the Association premises on Balestier Road during the period 2007–2008.

Bala recollects, how around the beginning of 2007, his good friend Purush (Purushotaman R, SIA member) persuaded him to return and actively participate in the activities of the Association. Though he had continued with his membership, the Association had somehow fallen out of his radar due to other professional priorities. To his surprise, Bala was to discover that over the past few years the Association had seen a steady decline. Some semblance of activity had continued in the sports department and the Association continued to be lauded for its hockey and cricket teams, but it did little else. What was more worrying was, the coffers were empty and what had once been the congregating point of the Indian community, had dwindled into a 'drunkard's den', avoided by women and families. Bala realised if corrective measures were to be taken, a person of some professional standing and with the capacity to raise funds needed to be roped in. It was around this time that he heard of Ambassador K Kesavapany, a diplomat and senior civil servant who had already served as Singapore's High Commissioner to Malaysia and Singapore's Permanent Representative to the UN in Geneva.

The duo first met at the Singapore Cricket Club. In the past, Ambassador Kesavapany had visited the SIA only on two occasions, both times to watch his son play cricket. But now he was persuaded by Bala to join as a member. Several closed-door meetings with SIA Committee Members followed, revealing the extent of the financial crisis the Association faced: not only was it running in deficit, taxes had not been paid for several years and a renovation of the premises would need an investment of at least SGD 500,000! In order to secure the loan, a team of 10 Members of SIA comprising Ambassador Kesavapany, V P Jothi, Eddie Raj, Haider Sithawalla, Krishna, Brigadier (Retd) Kirpa Ram Vij, M Rajaram, Dr Kamal Bose, Murali Pany and Shabbir Hassanbhai provided personal guarantee for a bank loan and refurbishment plans were drawn up and work was initiated.

In this regard Bala remains deeply appreciative of the contributions of not only Ambassador Kesavapany, present President of SIA, but also of senior corporate official and SIA Committee Member, V P Jothi as well as Eddie Raj and Krishna V, for planning and executing the renovation. As the ball was set rolling, the expenses climbed, and eventually the SIA incurred almost SGD 800,000 in refurbishment expenses. But fortunately, after some initial repayment by the SIA, S M Jaleel, Indian entrepreneur and philanthropist came forward and underwrote the balance loan. The timely intervention of Bala and his peers placed the SIA on a new trajectory of growth and social contribution: as Ambassador Kesavapany fondly reminiscences, when the Association was going through a low point in its history, it was Bala who kept faith and believed it could be salvaged. He knocked on many a door and stood at the end of many a social gathering holding the SIA membership form — new members brought in new ideas and the rest is history!

One of Bala's most recent engagements has been his involvement with SINDA (Singapore Indian Development Association) since its foundation in August 1991, with a single-minded purpose of uplifting the educational performance of the entire Indian community. SINDA is a direct fall-out of the Action Committee on Indian Education (ACIE) chaired by the respected civil servant, J Y Pillay and formed by the government of Singapore with an eclectic membership drawn from academia, civil service and the private sector. Long years ago G Kandasamy and pioneers like Bala had voiced their concern about the place of the Indian community in the fast evolving socio-economic scenario of Singapore. As the years progressed various interventions had been implemented till the establishment of the Indian Children Educational Task Force by the TRC in 1987. The report submitted by the Task Force, in the preparation of which Bala played an active role, would bring home to the government the enormity of the problem that the community had to contend with while stalwarts like S R Nathan, the future President of Singapore, G Kandasamy, S Dhanabalan, S Jayakumar, N Varaprasad and V Krishna would be vocal in pointing in the direction of the large Indian underclass.

In SINDA the long cherished dream of a National Committee for the educational advancement of the Indian children has been achieved and the 1996 report of SINDA's Executive Committee showed that the level of Indian students has in general improved and more importantly, there are suitable alternatives for students who do not qualify for the next level of education.[14] Today the self-help model of SINDA is cited as one of the role models for volunteer development in Singapore and the Best Volunteer Management Award was conferred on it in 2002. Bala has been involved in some of the landmark programmes like STEP or TEACH with SINDA, programmes which aim to supplement school programme by providing more personalised tuition. He enlisted himself as a volunteer and despite his advanced years, for nine years after the TEACH project was launched would visit students' homes on Sunday mornings to provide tuitions. Eventually he would be decorated by President S R Nathan as the oldest volunteer in SINDA!

Loss

Bala lost one of his closest friends, Kanda, in 1999. Since they first came to know each other in 1938, the two had fought shoulder to shoulder for many an issue they were passionate about. Subsequently, Kanda had given up his political office to devote his time entirely to the AUPE (Amalgamated Union of Public Employees). Even on the eve of his retirement in 1993 Kanda, a man who felt strong empathy for the cause of government staff and workers, had fought against the civil service medical scheme which he felt was unfair on poorly paid civil service employees. An amendment to the scheme suggested that civil servants would be required to make a co-payment towards medical expenses. However with the AUPE stepping in, the original scheme was continued and civil servants like Bala who had retired earlier and earned only a small pension continued to enjoy free medical services apart from the payment of a nominal fee at the time of admission to government hospitals.

But the following year Bala and Sumitra were to face yet another loss — a loss that they would struggle to reconcile with in the years to come. In the year 2000 they lost their only son Arjun. He was 27, at the prime of his youth, one who since childhood had been a bright, playful boy with a rare flare for writing like his father. Anidha recalls, with Arjun's birth their household had changed, it had seemed more fun, the strict discipline a little lax. If Bala had been firm it was only about his children's education, wanting to bequeath to them the academic edge he had missed himself. As parents Bala and Sumitra also encouraged their children to pursue extra-curricular activities: while Anidha took to Bharatnatyam, Arjun, like his father, turned out to be a keen sports enthusiast, representing his college in soccer, rugby and tennis. In academics his preferred subject was English in which he excelled, winning the college award for excellent performance in English Literature in 1992. But that was a period when study of the Humanities held out little in terms of career prospect in Singapore, the focus being largely on medicine and mathematics. Though keen to study law, securing admission in the universities of Singapore proved to be difficult and eventually, Arjun decided to move to Australia to study finance.

On his return to Singapore after the final exams, Arjun would seem happy, spending a lot of time with Anidha, her husband John Thomas and his many friends in the city. The end when it came would be sudden, taking the family by utter dismay.

Conclusion

Bala's daughter Anidha recalls, her mother and she were not allowed the time to grieve after Arjun's death. Her father ensured within a week the family was back at their work places. Sounds too pragmatic, perhaps heartless? If asked, Bala says he had resigned himself to the realms of Omar Khayyam and quotes from the poet's quatrain 52:

> "And that inverted bowl we call
> The sky,
> Whereunder crawling coop't
> We live and die,
> Lift not thy hands to It for
> Help — for It
> Rolls impotently on as Thou
> Or I."

Earlier, if he had planned the education of Anidha and Arjun, now with equal meticulousness he planned for countless others and continued to assiduously help his friend R O Daniel in the preparation of the short history of the Singapore Indian Education Trust which was incidentally published in 2002.

In fact this aspect of Bala's character, a side that is deeply nurturing of the future generations is particularly endearing. He realised early the shortcomings of his own childhood and youth and endeavoured to fill in those gaps for the coming generations of Indians in Singapore, much as an artist fills his canvas with colour. If he was deprived from the beauty of Indian art forms for most of his early life, he tried to bridge the gap in Singapore through his work with SIFAS. He familiarised himself as best as he could with the classic dance forms of Bharatanatyam and Kathak so that he could make serious contributions to the SIFAS syllabus and teaching methods. If he felt he knew little about the real roots of Hinduism, growing up as he did amidst a more ritualistic practice of the religion, he tried to correct it through initiating spiritual lectures conducted by the HEB Education Sub-committee. If he felt as a second generation Indian, he had taken time to know himself and grow in confidence, he took pragmatic steps by which the current generation could be put in touch with their cultural roots early in their life.

Bala, along with other members of his community, has struggled with two fears in a fast evolving Singapore. Firstly that the vast Indian underclass will not be able to keep up with the demands of meritocracy: much as meritocracy is desirable to provide equal opportunities in a multiracial society, that it would emerge as a threat to some in the Indian community. And secondly, there are apprehensions that the Tamil language will die a natural death in the absence of state-driven inducement to study the language. Again, Bala has dealt with these problems in his own way. Not only has he contributed time and effort at the macro level, but he has also broken down and delineated his own responsibilities at the micro level as he did when he and his colleagues organised breakfast for the students under the TRC–EAP scheme. Sumitra also recalls his leaving home diligently at 7am every Sunday while a volunteer with SINDA. Despite his advanced years, he has not missed an opportunity to tutor the children of whom he has taken responsibility, often taking Ladybird books from his children's personal collection to read to them so their English improves. Both Bala and Sumitra have continued to keep in touch with the children he helped tutor during his lifetime, their accomplishments as adults providing them with undiluted happiness today.

But along with such strong positives, some worrying signs remain. One wonders if he ever feels perturbed by the gradually changing political ethos of Singapore, even as Socialism, the political credo with which he made a beginning as a trade unionist, gradually erodes away and the island seems inhospitable to the poor? When for example the Rent Conciliation Board was abolished, did it bother him that it marked the end of one of the few ways the underprivileged could seek legal action? Or when he joined the Singapore Pools, did it worry him that the company might indulge a national addiction to gambling, despite the protestations by the government that it was a way of giving legal vent to a common vice? Or that even as he and his peers work hard so that the Tamil language and culture remain extant, they perhaps do so at the cost of the many sub-groups which comprise the Indian community of Singapore? That while the Tamils form the biggest group (64%) of a minority community, there are many sub-groups for whom mother tongue study is not offered as an option by national schools from primary to pre-university level? That there might be need of creating an enhanced infrastructure for non-Tamil Indian languages (abbreviated as NTIL by the Education Ministry) as well? While pioneers like Bala bemoan the lack of integration between the Indian community of Singapore and first generation Indian migrants, perhaps more work needs to be done in cultural exchange and achieving a community image that is more cosmopolitan and inclusive?

Personally if Bala has any lasting regrets, it is about the Hindu Endowments Board. He feels that despite his long association with the Hindu temples from 1961 to 1981, he and his peers have been able to make little headway in forging together a well-conceived social welfare plan and having it executed. He feels strongly that temple funds should be more effectively utilised for providing welfare and support to needy Hindu families and for this a more structured intervention (perhaps appointing a professional Welfare Officer and publishing a periodical bulletin of the temple's welfare services) would prove helpful.

But such interventions can be left in the safe custody of the future generations, the same generations that Bala and his compatriots have painstakingly nurtured. For the time being the most enduring image of Bala is of him sitting in the shaded veranda of his La Salle Street house; the air fills with the solemn tolling of a bell from a nearby church, an earnest biographer sits before him recording his responses. In the room behind him is a freshly garlanded photograph of Arjun. For Bala just as that portrait is true, so is his daughter Anidha who lives her life in modern-day Singapore, a life that is very different from his own. His two granddaughters, Hannah Divya (18 years) and Jemima Amritha (15 years), the fourth generation living in Singapore, are as comfortable conversing in Tamil as they are in English. In SINDA the Indian community has achieved what they had long-aspired for — a government endorsed organisation for the academic enhancement of the Indian community. He repeatedly questions if his life is worthy of documentation. He knows that some of the ideals by which he has led his life have gradually lost their relevance even as they are achieved. He has devoted his life to a mission of providing the Indian community of Singapore with a strong sense of identity. But today, as the new 'Singaporean' identity emerges, hasn't the old mission lost some of its sparkle? With integrated communities living in high-rise apartment blocks and new associational and communal neighbourhood interaction networks, hasn't the maintenance of CMIO generated pluralism become gradually irrelevant?[15]

A distant look comes into Bala's eyes. He seems to see far into the future… Ever an admirer of literature, he quotes Ben Jonson and the flower of light leaves a lingering fragrance:

> "It is not growing like a tree
> In bulk doth make Man better be;
> Or standing long an oak, three hundred year,
> To fall a log at last, dry, bald, and sere:
> A lily of a day,
> Is fairer far in May,
> Although it fall and die that night-
> It was the plant and flower of light.
> In small proportions we just beauties see;
> And in short measures life may perfect be."

Notes

[1] *A History of Modern Singapore: 1819–2005*, C M Turnbull. NUS Press, Singapore, 1989, p. 326.

[2] *Passage of Indians: 1923–2003*. SIA, Singapore, 2003, p. 180.

[3] Ibid, pp. 180–182.

[4] Ibid., p. 163, 165.

[5] Singapore Income Tax Act, cap141, part xii, p. 89.

[6] *Language, Nation and Development in Southeast Asia*. Eds Lee Hock Guan and Leo Suryadinata. ISEAS, Singapore, 2007. *The Multilingual State in Search of the*

Nation: The Language Policy and Discourse in Singapore's Nation Building, Eugene K B Tan. ISEAS, Singapore, 2007.

[7] *My Lifelong Challenge: Singapore's Bilingual Journey*, Lew Kuan Yew. Straits Times Press, Singapore, 2012, p. 51.

[8] *The Multilingual State in Search of the Nation: The Language Policy and Discourse in Singapore's Nation Building*. Eugene K B Tan, p. 78.

[9] *My Lifelong Challenge: Singapore's Bilingual Journey*, Lew Kuan Yew. Straits Times Press, Singapore, 2012, p. 63.

[10] Ibid., p. 70.

[11] Sangam literature dates back to the period between 500 BC and 200 AD when Tamil literacy societies (Sangams) formed, and patronised by royalty, consisted of eminent poets and intellectuals who congregated in a special mandapam in the royal palace and discussed aspects of the government, politics and debated philosophy.

[12] Information on SIET, *Singapore Indian Education* Trust: *The First Thirty Years*, R O Daniel. Stamford Press, Singapore, 2002.

[13] *From Red Dot to Republic*, by M Bala Subramanion, *Tabla!*, Singapore, 27 March 2015, pp. 2–3.

[14] Information on SINDA, *Singapore Indian Education Trust: The First Thirty Years*, R O Daniel. Stamford Press, Singapore, 2002, p. 52. Also *A Place in the Community: SINDA at 20, Looking Back, Moving Forward*. Audrey Perera. Singapore Indian Development Association, Singapore, 2011.

[15] CMIO refers to the *Chinese, Malay, Indian, Others* model of Singapore.

Post Office Memories

1973. Bala with Bertie Cheng (at the time, General Manager) and staff of POSB.
Standing. Extreme right: Bertie Cheng.
Sitting. Centre: Bala.

2000. At the opening of SingPost at Jalan Eunos. *From left: Lee Shin Koi, Wong Lee Hoong, Bala and William Tan, at the time the CEO of SingPost.*

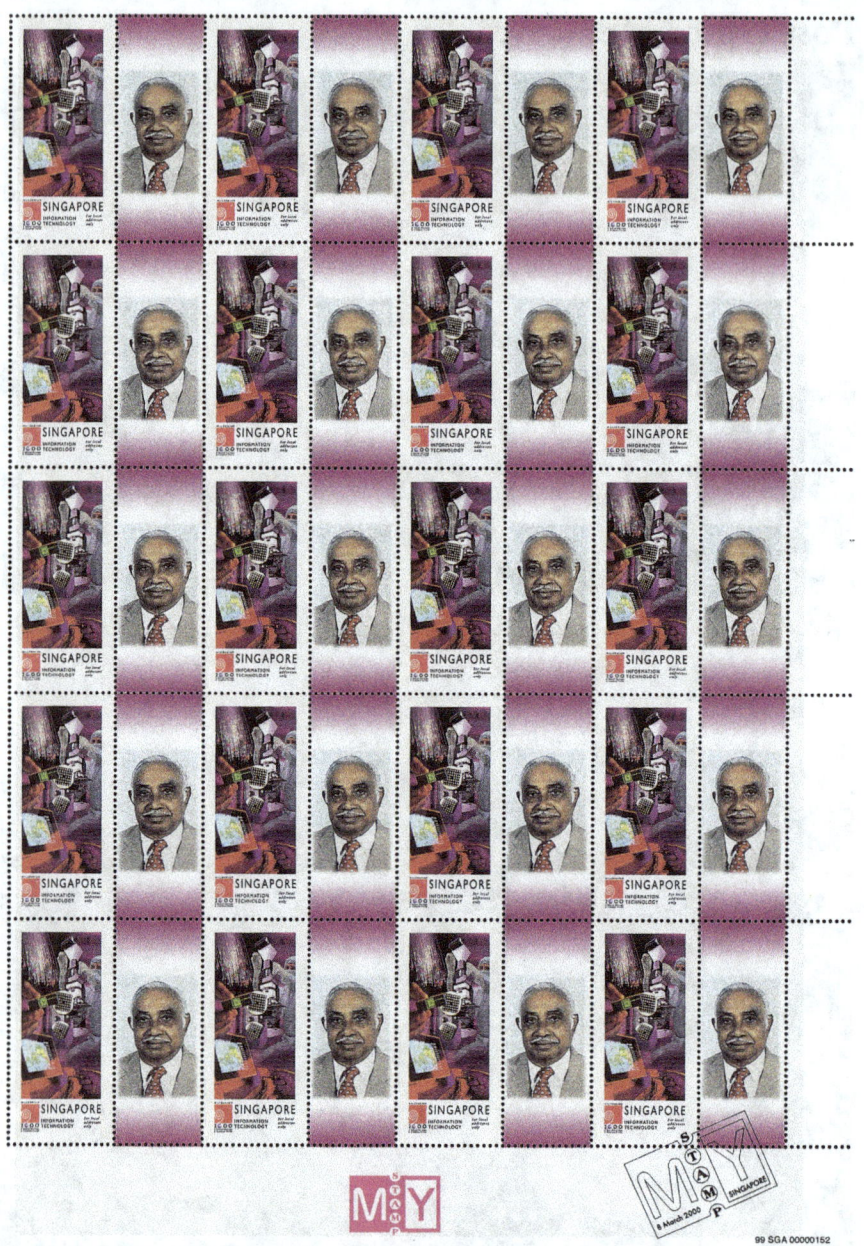

2000. "My Stamp" printed at the inauguration of the SingPost Centre at Jalan Eunos.

2010. Get-together of the postal group. *Sitting. From left: Bala, Wong Lee Hoong, Low Siow Chek. Standing. From left: Lee Chow Soon, Bertie Cheng.*

8th July 2010. Minister Lui Tuck Yew at the Opening Ceremony of the Fullerton Heritage Gallery at Fullerton Hotel. With him are Giovanni Viterale, General Manager at the Fullerton Hotel, Bala, Sumitra and staff.

20th April 2013. The Singapore Memory Project. Bala and Sumitra with former and current SingPost staff at Fullerton Heritage Gallery at the Fullerton Hotel.

23rd September 2013. Bala with current President of Singapore Dr Tony Tan Keng Yam and Mary Tan on the occasion of SingPost's Gift to the Nation, held at the Fullerton Heritage Gallery in the Fullerton Hotel. *From left: Mary Tan and Dr Tony Tan (foreground), Giovanni Viterale, General Manager at the Fullerton Hotel, Bala and Sumitra.*

20th July 2015. Bala with then Minister of State, Ministry of Culture, Community and Youth, Sam Tan Chin Siong for the official opening of The Singapore Journey: 50 Years Through Stamps, held at the Singapore Philatelic Museum. *From left: Woo Keng Leong (Senior Executive Vice President/Head of Postal Services of SingPost), William Tan, Wong Lee Hoong, Sam Tan, Bala, Professor Cheah Jin Seng, Rosa Daniel (CEO, National Heritage Board) and Tresnawati Prihadi (General Manager, Singapore Philatelic Museum).*

7th December 2015. Bala and Sumitra meet the current Prime Minister of Singapore Lee Hsien Loong at a function gazetting the Fullerton Hotel as a National Monument. Image courtesy of PM Lee Hsien Loong's Facebook page.

1972 and Beyond

1975. Bala entertaining SIFAS Committee Members at home. *From left: Bala, Dr V S Rajan, A Sachithanandan, A M Cherian, I S Menon, S Gopinathan, D Natarajan. Lady in sari was an examiner at SIFAS. The child is Bala and Sumitra's son Arjun.*

1992. Indian community dinner for Senior Minister Lee Kuan Yew. *From left: Satpal Khattar, V Krishna, Gopinath Pillai, Bala.*

28th August 1999. Bala receives the Long Service Award from V M Shaw (of Shaw Brothers) on the 50th Anniversary of SIFAS.

August 2005. Bala receives an award from the 6th President of Singapore S R Nathan in connection with SINDA's Read Project.

2009. Bala receives an award from the then Minister for Finance Tharman Shanmugaratnam in appreciation of contributions to Sri Mariamman Temple. *From left: HEB Member Dr T Chandroo, then Minister for Finance Tharman Shanmugaratnam, then HEB Chairman S Rajendran, Bala.*

2011. Bala garlands Former President of India Dr A P J Abdul Kalam at SIA. Behind Kalam stands K Kesavapany, then Director of the Institute of Southeast Asian Studies, Singapore.

Fond Moments with Family

1977. Bala with his family at their home in La Salle Street.

We Must Make a People

1991. Bala with his sister Sulochana, wife Sumitra and niece Gomathy.

August 1995. Bala's daughter Anidha's wedding reception at the Hyatt Hotel, Singapore.

1997. Bala with his sister Chandra Bai in Thanjavur, India.

2012, Bangalore. Sumitra's family, or Bala's "fond outlaws". *From left: A Kesavan, A Chandran, Professor A Appan, Sumitra, Shobana Subramani, A Anandan, Ashok Appan.*

2015. A family gathering of three generations. *From left: Sumitra, Divya, Anidha, Amritha, Bala, John.*

www.ingramcontent.com/pod-product-compliance
Lightning Source LLC
Chambersburg PA
CBHW052056230426
43662CB00037B/1932